At Issue

Do Cell Phones Cause Cancer?

Other Books in the At Issue Series:

At Issue

Do Cell Phones Cause Cancer?

Clay Farris Naff, Book Editor

GREENHAVEN PRESS
A part of Gale, Cengage Learning

GALE
CENGAGE Learning·

Detroit • New York • San Francisco • New Haven, Conn • Waterville, Maine • London

Elizabeth Des Chenes, *Director, Publishing Solutions*

© 2013 Greenhaven Press, a part of Gale, Cengage Learning.

Gale and Greenhaven Press are registered trademarks used herein under license.

For more information, contact:
Greenhaven Press
27500 Drake Rd.
Farmington Hills, MI 48331-3535
Or you can visit our Internet site at www.gale.cengage.com

For product information and technology assistance, contact us at

Gale Customer Support, 1-800-877-4253
For permission to use material from this text or product, submit all requests online at www.cengage.com/permissions

Further permissions questions can be e-mailed to permissionrequest@cengage.com

Articles in Greenhaven Press anthologies are often edited for length to meet page requirements. In addition, original titles of these works are changed to clearly present the main thesis and to explicitly indicate the author's opinion. Every effort is made to ensure that Greenhaven Press accurately reflects the original intent of the authors. Every effort has been made to trace the owners of copyrighted material.

Cover image © Images.com/Corbis.

LIBRARY OF CONGRESS CATALOGING-IN-PUBLICATION DATA

Do cell phones cause cancer? / Clay Farris Naff, book editor.
    pages cm. -- (At issue)
    Includes bibliographical references and index.
    ISBN 978-0-7377-6167-2 (hardcover) -- ISBN 978-0-7377-6168-9 (pbk.)
    1. Cell phone systems--Health aspects. 2. Cell phones--Health aspects. 3. Radio waves--Health aspects. 4. Carcinogenesis. I. Naff, Clay Farris.
    RA569.3.D58 2013
    612'.014481--dc23
                                                            2012051704

Printed in the United States of America
1 2 3 4 5 6 7 17 16 15 14 13

Contents

Introduction

Sheryl Crow has talent, fame, and fortune. She also has a brain tumor.

The nine-time Grammy Award-winning singer believes she knows why. Speaking to television journalist Katie Couric, Crow said she blames radiation from her cell phone for the tumor in her head.

"I do have the theory that it's related to that," she said, "because in the early days when I was promoting my first record, I did hours of phoners [phone interviews] on the old, archaic cell phones."[1]

It sounds plausible, and some scientists would surely say that cell phone radiation cannot be ruled out.

However, like the issue of cell phone radiation and brain cancer itself, the story of Crow's tumor is more complicated than it first appears. For one thing, Crow previously had breast cancer. No one thinks that her cell phone caused that, and no one can say whether her breast cancer is somehow related to the growth in her brain. For another, Crow's own doctor doubts that cell phone radiation causes brain cancer.

By its very nature, cancer resists discovery of its particular cause. With a communicable disease, such as the flu, it is relatively easy to determine the cause. If a certain virus is present the disease may be found; absent the virus there is no disease. But cancer comes about when the DNA in a cell of one's own body mutates, allowing that cell to go rogue and multiply rapidly without any benefit to the body. The precise cause of that one particular mutation can be impossible to discover. It could be the result of a cosmic ray, or a chemical contaminant in something that unlucky person ate, or even just a random quantum event.

The only reliable way to discover what causes cancer and what does not is statistical. There are two general approaches to this method: experimental and epidemiological. In the first, cells or animals related to humans are exposed to a possible carcinogen under controlled experimental conditions. If cancer develops in the experimental group and does not develop in the control group, then scientists infer that they may have discovered a carcinogen. That, for example, is how tobacco was found to cause cancer.

Epidemiology is the study of patterns of disease in a large population. It can be very useful for pointing scientists toward the cause of a particular disease, especially cancer. For example, if epidemiologists find that asthma rates vary in a non-random way between modern urban settings and underdeveloped rural settings, then scientists can begin to look at the differences in the two environments to try to find a cause. On the flipside, if epidemiology finds no variation in the incidence of a disease when an environmental factor does vary, scientists may conclude that the factor in question is not a cause of the disease.

There is one other common way that people infer cause for a disease: correlation. In many everyday experiences correlation gives us important information. For example, the old saying that where there's smoke, there's fire generally holds true. However, correlation is not scientific evidence of cause. The reason is simple: in many instances correlation does not indicate cause. To return to the example of tobacco and cancer, correlation would show that people who carry lighters tend to develop cancer, but that would not be evidence that lighters cause cancer.

Correlation is what led people to ask if cell phone radiation might be causing brain cancer in the first place. As cell phones proliferated, some people who used them developed brain cancer. Questions were raised about a possible causal link. That prompted some researchers to conduct lab experiments, with controversial results. Some scientists believe the experiments indicate a hazard in cell phone radiation. Others strongly dispute that. To date, the epidemiological evidence generally shows no association between cell phone use and the incidence of brain cancer.

But the controversy within the medical establishment has spilled over into the public arena. For example, Denise Amrich, a registered nurse, has written in the ZDNet Health blog: "Cell phones are now up there with lead, engine exhaust, coffee, and chloroform. I mean, call me crazy, but I feel a lot safer placing a call on my iPhone (maybe with a nice cup of Joe in the other hand) than I would snacking on the paint chips from my grandparent's window sills, or breathing in the black cloudy fumes billowing from a belching tailpipe."[2]

Amrich notes a paradox in the public discourse about carcinogenic hazards in new technologies: on the one hand, the dangers inherent in new discoveries often remain concealed until real harm has been done. Marie Curie, for example, the co-discoverer of radium, had no idea that by carrying the stuff around in vials on her person she was dooming herself to a premature death of cancer. Similarly, technicians who worked with early x-ray machines had no idea that they were also putting their lives in danger.

On the other hand, in recent decades there has been a tendency to sound the alarm about cancer danger in all sorts of things, some of which lacked any basis in evidence. Tongue in cheek, Amrich writes, "Doesn't everything cause cancer?"

No one really believes that everything causes cancer. However, the World Health Organization and a number of reputable doctors and medical researchers consider the question of whether cell phone radiation causes brain cancer to be unsolved. By contrast, most experts in radiation and many reputable doctors and medical researchers consider the question not worth worrying about.

For singer Crow, the news is relatively good. Whatever the cause, her tumor appears to be noncancerous. Meantime, despite the unwelcome lump in her skull, Crow says she feels healthy and happy.

Notes

1. KTLA News, "Singer Sheryl Crow Says Cell Phone Caused Her Brain Tumor," September 11, 2012. http://www.ktla.com/news/landing/ktla-sheryl-crow brain-tumor-couric-show,0,4797318.story.
2. Denise Amrich, "It's Official: Your Cell Phone May Cause Cancer," ZDNet Health, June 2, 2011. http://www.zdnet.com/blog/health/its-official-your-cell-phone-may-cause-cancer/233.

1

Cell Phones May Be Carcinogenic Hazards

Danielle Dellorto

Danielle Dellorto is a senior medical producer at CNN, and also works as a writer and contributor at CNN Health.

The World Health Organization (WHO) has categorized cell phones as being at the carcinogenic risk level of lead, engine exhaust, and chloroform. This report comes despite repeated previous assurances by the agency that the microwave radiation emitted by mobile phones posed no physical risk to the public. The warning is not, however, a confirmation of cell phone radiation as a carcinogen, but rather an admittance that research results conducted by programs, such as the National Institutes of Health, are thus far not conclusively negative. Consumers that are concerned may implement cautious cell phone use by limiting talk time, keeping a short distance between their phone and ear during use, and taking advantage of texting or earpiece devices.

Radiation from cell phones can possibly cause cancer, according to the World Health Organization. The agency now lists mobile phone use in the same "carcinogenic hazard" category as lead, engine exhaust and chloroform.

Before its announcement Tuesday, WHO had assured consumers that no adverse health effects had been established.

A team of 31 scientists from 14 counties, including the United States, made the decision after reviewing peer-reviewed studies on cell phone safety. The team found enough evidence to categorize personal exposure as "possibly carcinogenic to humans."

What that means is they found some evidence of increase in glioma and acoustic neuroma brain cancer for mobile phone users, but have not been able to draw conclusions for other types of cancers.

"The biggest problem we have is that we know most environmental factors take several decades of exposure before we really see the consequences," said Dr. Keith Black, chairman of neurology at Cedars-Sinai Medical Center in Los Angeles.

Studies Remain Inconclusive

The type of radiation coming out of a cell phone is called non-ionizing. It is not like an X-ray, but more like a very low-powered microwave oven.

"What microwave radiation does in most simplistic terms is similar to what happens to food in microwaves, essentially cooking the brain," Black said. "So in addition to leading to a development of cancer and tumors, there could be a whole host of other effects like cognitive memory function, since the memory temporal lobes are where we hold our cell phones."

Wireless industry responded to Tuesday's announcement saying it "does not mean cell phones cause cancer."

CTIA-The Wireless Association added that WHO researchers "did not conduct any new research, but rather reviewed published studies."

The European Environmental Agency has pushed for more studies, saying cell phones could be as big a public health risk as smoking, asbestos and leaded gasoline. The head of a prominent cancer-research institute at the University of Pittsburgh sent a memo to all employees urging them to limit cell phone use because of a possible risk of cancer.

"When you look at cancer development—particularly brain cancer—it takes a long time to develop. I think it is a good idea to give the public some sort of warning that long-term exposure to radiation from your cell phone could possibly cause cancer," said Dr. Henry Lai, research professor in bioengineering at University of Washington who has studied radiation for more than 30 years.

A study by researchers at the National Institutes of Health revealed radiation emitted after just 50 minutes on a mobile phone increases the activity in brain cells.

Results from the largest international study on cell phones and cancer was released in 2010. It showed participants in the study who used a cell phone for 10 years or more had doubled the rate of brain glioma, a type of tumor. To date, there have been no long-term studies on the effects of cell phone usage among children.

"Children's skulls and scalps are thinner. So the radiation can penetrate deeper into the brain of children and young adults. Their cells are dividing at a faster rate, so the impact of radiation can be much larger," said Black of Cedars-Sinai Medical Center.

In February, a study by researchers at the National Institutes of Health revealed radiation emitted after just 50 minutes on a mobile phone increases the activity in brain cells. The effects of brain activity being artificially stimulated are still unknown.

Neurosurgeon and CNN chief medical correspondent Dr. Sanjay Gupta says Tuesday's announcement, "dealt a blow to those who have long said, 'There is no possible mechanism for cell phones to cause cancer.' By classifying cell phones as a possible carcinogen, they also seem to be tacitly admitting a mechanism could exist."

Ways to Lower Risk

Manufacturers of many popular cell phones already warn consumers to keep their device away from their body and medical experts say there are other ways to minimize cell phone radiation.

The Apple iPhone 4 safety manual says users' radiation exposure should not exceed FCC guidelines: "When using iPhone near your body for voice calls or for wireless data transmission over a cellular network, keep iPhone at least 15 millimeters (5/8 inch) away from the body."

BlackBerry Bold advises users to "keep the BlackBerry device at least 0.98 inch (25 millimeters) from your body when the BlackBerry device is transmitting."

The logic behind such recommendations is that the further the phone is from the body, the less radiation is absorbed. Users can also use the speakerphone function or a wired earpiece to gain some distance.

Users can text instead of talk if they want to keep the phone away from their faces.

Finally, cell phones emit the most radiation when they are attempting to connect to cellular towers. A moving phone, or a phone in an area with a weak signal, has to work harder, giving off more radiation. So users can avoid using their cell phones in elevators, buildings and rural areas if they want to reduce their exposure, experts say.

2

No Definitive Evidence
Ties Cell Phone Radiation to
Brain Cancer

National Cancer Institute

The National Cancer Institute is part of the National Institutes of Health (NIH), established by Congress in 1937. Responsibilities of the program include conducting and supporting cancer research nationwide, the training and educating of scientists and physicians, and disseminating information about cancer to the general public.

As cell phone use has become more widespread throughout the United States, with over three hundred million mobile phone subscribers in 2010, concerns over the safety of these devices have also increased. Radiofrequency, the kind of radiation produced by cell phone use, is a form of non-ionizing energy. While radiofrequency energy is known to cause cells in organisms to speed, or heat, up, damage to DNA has not been documented, which therefore eliminates cancer as a possible effect. Several studies have been conducted to investigate any links between cell phone use and brain cancers, including the INTERPHONE and Danish Cancer Registry studies. While precise statistics were inconclusive, no direct association was discovered.

National Cancer Institute, "Cell Phones and Cancer Risk," *National Cancer Institute at the National Institutes of Health*, October 24, 2011.

There are three main reasons why people are concerned that cell phones (also known as "wireless" or "mobile" telephones) might have the potential to cause certain types of cancer or other health problems:

- Cell phones emit radiofrequency energy (radio waves), a form of non-ionizing radiation. Tissues nearest to where the phone is held can absorb this energy.

- The number of cell phone users has increased rapidly. As of 2010, there were more than 303 million subscribers to cell phone service in the United States, according to the Cellular Telecommunications and Internet Association. This is a nearly threefold increase from the 110 million users in 2000. Globally, the number of cell phone subscriptions is estimated by the International Telecommunications Union to be 5 billion.

- Over time, the number of cell phone calls per day, the length of each call, and the amount of time people use cell phones have increased. Cell phone technology has also undergone substantial changes.

To date there is no evidence from studies of cells, animals, or humans that radiofrequency energy can cause cancer.

The Effects of Radiofrequency Energy

Radiofrequency energy is a form of electromagnetic radiation. Electromagnetic radiation can be categorized into two types: ionizing (e.g., x-rays, radon, and cosmic rays) and non-ionizing (e.g., radiofrequency and extremely low-frequency or power frequency).

Exposure to ionizing radiation, such as from radiation therapy, is known to increase the risk of cancer. However, although many studies have examined the potential health effects of non-ionizing radiation from radar, microwave ovens, and other sources, there is currently no consistent evidence that non-ionizing radiation increases cancer risk.

The only known biological effect of radiofrequency energy is heating. The ability of microwave ovens to heat food is one example of this effect of radiofrequency energy. Radiofrequency exposure from cell phone use does cause heating; however, it is not sufficient to measurably increase body temperature.

A recent study showed that when people used a cell phone for 50 minutes, brain tissues on the same side of the head as the phone's antenna metabolized more glucose than did tissues on the opposite side of the brain. The researchers noted that the results are preliminary, and possible health outcomes from this increase in glucose metabolism are still unknown. . . .

Research Is Unable to Tie Radiofrequency Energy to Cancer

Although there have been some concerns that radiofrequency energy from cell phones held closely to the head may affect the brain and other tissues, to date there is no evidence from studies of cells, animals, or humans that radiofrequency energy can cause cancer.

It is generally accepted that damage to DNA is necessary for cancer to develop. However, radiofrequency energy, unlike ionizing radiation, does not cause DNA damage in cells, and it has not been found to cause cancer in animals or to enhance the cancer-causing effects of known chemical carcinogens in animals.

Researchers have carried out several types of epidemiologic studies to investigate the possibility of a relationship between cell phone use and the risk of malignant (cancerous) brain tumors, such as gliomas, as well as benign (noncancerous) tumors, such as acoustic neuromas (tumors in the cells of the nerve responsible for hearing), most meningiomas (tumors in the meninges, membranes that cover and protect the brain and spinal cord), and parotid gland tumors (tumors in the salivary glands).

Most published analyses from [the Interphone Study] have shown no statistically significant increases in brain or central nervous system cancers related to higher amounts of cell phone use.

In one type of study, called a case-control study, cell phone use is compared between people with these types of tumors and people without them. In another type of study, called a cohort study, a large group of people is followed over time and the rate of these tumors in people who did and didn't use cell phones is compared. Cancer incidence data can also be analyzed over time to see if the rates of cancer changed in large populations during the time that cell phone use increased dramatically. The results of these studies have generally not provided clear evidence of a relationship between cell phone use and cancer, but there have been some statistically significant findings in certain subgroups of people.

Findings from specific research studies are summarized below:

- The Interphone Study, conducted by a consortium of researchers from 13 countries, is the largest health-related case-control study of use of cell phones and head and neck tumors. Most published analyses from this study have shown no statistically significant increases in brain or central nervous system cancers related to higher amounts of cell phone use. One recent analysis showed a statistically significant, albeit modest, increase in the risk of glioma among the small proportion of study participants who spent the most total time on cell phone calls. However, the researchers considered this finding inconclusive because they felt that the amount of use reported by some respondents was unlikely and because the participants who reported lower levels of use appeared to have a reduced risk of brain cancer. Another recent study from the group found no relationship between brain tumor locations and regions of the brain that were exposed to the highest level of radiofrequency energy from cell phones.

- A cohort study in Denmark linked billing information from more than 358,000 cell phone subscribers with brain tumor incidence data from the Danish Cancer Registry. The analyses found no association between cell phone use and the incidence of glioma, meningioma, or acoustic neuroma, even among people who had been cell phone subscribers for 13 or more years.

- Early case-control studies in the United States, Europe, and Japan were unable to demonstrate a relationship between cell phone use and glioma or meningioma.

- Some case-control studies in Sweden found statistically significant trends of increasing brain cancer risk for the total amount of cell phone use and the years of use among people who began using cell phones before age 20. However, another large, case-control study in Sweden did not find an increased risk of brain cancer among people between the ages of 20 and 69. In addition, the international CE-FALO study, which compared children who were diagnosed with brain cancer between ages 7 and 19 with similar children who were not, found no relationship between their cell phone use and risk for brain cancer.

- NCI's Surveillance, Epidemiology, and End Results (SEER) Program, which tracks cancer incidence in the United States over time, found no increase in the incidence of brain or other central nervous system cancers between 1987 and 2007, despite the dramatic increase in cell phone use in this country during that time. Similarly, incidence data from Denmark, Finland, Norway, and Sweden for the period 1974–2008 revealed no increase in age-adjusted incidence of brain tumors. A 2012 study by NCI researchers, which compared observed glioma incidence rates in SEER with projected rates based on risks observed in the Interphone study, found that the projected rates were consistent with observed U.S. rates. The researchers also compared the SEER rates with projected rates based on a Swedish study published in 2011. They determined that the projected rates were at least 40 percent higher than, and incompatible with, the actual U.S. rates.

- Studies of workers exposed to radiofrequency energy have shown no evidence of increased risk of brain tumors among U.S. Navy electronics technicians, aviation technicians, or fire control technicians, those working in an electromagnetic pulse test program, plastic-ware workers, cellular phone manufacturing workers, or Navy personnel with a high probability of exposure to radar.

Bias and Flawed Methods Cause Inconsistencies

A limited number of studies have shown some evidence of statistical association of cell phone use and brain tumor risks, but most studies have found no association. Reasons for these discrepancies include the following:

- **Recall bias**, which may happen when a study collects data about prior habits and exposures using questionnaires administered after disease has been diagnosed in some of the study participants. It is possible that study participants who have brain tumors may remember their cell phone use differently than individuals without brain tumors. Many epidemiologic studies of cell phone use and brain cancer risk lack verifiable data about the total amount of cell phone use over time. In addition, people who develop a brain tumor may have a tendency to recall using their cell phone mostly on the same side of their head where the tumor was found, regardless of whether they actually used their phone on that side of their head a lot or only a little.

- **Inaccurate reporting**, which may happen when people say that something has happened more or less often than it actually did. People may not remember how much they used cell phones in a given time period.

- **Morbidity and mortality** among study participants who have brain cancer. Gliomas are particularly difficult to study, for example, because of their high death rate and the short survival of people who develop these tumors. Patients who survive initial treatment are often impaired, which may affect their responses to questions. Furthermore, for people who have died, next-of-kin are often less familiar with the cell phone use patterns of their deceased family member and may not accurately describe their patterns of use to an interviewer.

- **Participation bias**, which can happen when people who are diagnosed with brain tumors are more likely than healthy people (known as controls) to enroll in a research study. Also, controls who did not or rarely used cell phones were less likely to participate in the Interphone study than controls who used cell phones regularly. For example, the Interphone study reported participation rates of 78 percent for meningioma patients (range 56–92 percent for the individual studies), 64 percent for the glioma patients (range 36–92 percent), and 53 percent for control subjects (range 42–74 percent). One series of Swedish studies reported participation rates of 85 percent in people with brain cancer and 84 percent in control subjects.

- **Changing technology and methods of use.** Older studies evaluated radiofrequency energy exposure from analog cell phones. However, most cell phones today use digital technology, which operates at a different frequency and a lower power level than analog phones. Digital cell phones have been in use for more than a decade in the United States, and cellular technology continues to change. Texting, for example, has become a popular way of using a cell phone to communicate that does not require bringing the phone close to the head. Furthermore, the use of hands-free technology, such as wired and wireless headsets, is increasing and may decrease radiofrequency energy exposure to the head and brain.

Expert Organizations Find No Cell Phone-Cancer Link

The International Agency for Research on Cancer (IARC), a component of the World Health Organization, has recently classified radiofrequency fields as "possibly carcinogenic to humans," based on limited evidence from human studies, limited evidence from studies of radiofrequency energy and cancer in rodents, and weak mechanistic evidence (from studies of genotoxicity, effects on immune system function, gene and protein expression, cell signaling, oxidative stress, and apoptosis, along with studies of the possible effects of radiofrequency energy on the blood-brain barrier).

The American Cancer Society (ACS) states that the IARC classification means that there could be some risk associated with cancer, but the evidence is not strong enough to be considered causal and needs to be investigated further. Individuals who are concerned about radiofrequency exposure can limit their exposure, including using an ear piece and limiting cell phone use, particularly among children.

The Federal Communications Commission (FCC) concludes that there is no scientific evidence that proves that wireless phone use can lead to cancer or to other health problems, including headaches, dizziness, or memory loss.

The National Institute of Environmental Health Sciences (NIEHS) states that the weight of the current scientific evidence has not conclusively linked cell phone use with any adverse health problems, but more research is needed.

The U.S. Food and Drug Administration (FDA), which is responsible for regulating the safety of machines and devices that emit radiation (including cell phones), notes that studies reporting biological changes associated with radiofrequency energy have failed to be replicated and that the majority of human epidemiologic studies have failed to show a relationship between exposure to radiofrequency energy from cell phones and health problems.

The U.S. Centers for Disease Control and Prevention (CDC) states that, although some studies have raised concerns about the possible risks of cell phone use, scientific research as a whole does not support a statistically significant association between cell phone use and health effects.

The Federal Communications Commission (FCC) concludes that there is no scientific evidence that proves that wireless phone use can lead to cancer or to other health problems, including headaches, dizziness, or memory loss.

3

Cell Phone Radiation Affects Fetal Mice

Steven Reinberg

Steven Reinberg is a reporter and regular contributor for Health-Day, an online news service that provides daily health news to both consumers and medical professionals.

When exposed in utero to the radiation from a transmitting cell phone, mice appeared to display symptoms similar to attention deficit disorder in adulthood. The hypothesis of the experiment conducted by the team of Dr. Hugh Taylor is that the developing brain is likely more sensitive to external factors. While a direct link between the symptoms displayed by the mice cannot be made to humans, the study indicates the possibility of cell phone exposure having effects on people. The research, still in its earliest stages, warrants further study.

In experiments involving mice, fetal exposure to cellphone radiation appeared linked to symptoms in offspring that resemble attention-deficit hyperactivity disorder (ADHD) in human children, Yale researchers report.

Moreover, these problems with attention, hyperactivity and memory continued when the mice became adults and were worse the longer they were exposed to cellphone radiation in the womb, the researchers said.

Study Focuses on the Developing Brain

"The hypothesis was that the developing brain might be more susceptible to these types of insults," said senior researcher Dr. Hugh Taylor, a professor and chief of the division of reproductive endocrinology and infertility in the department of obstetrics, gynecology & reproductive sciences.

"We found they seem to have behavioral changes like ADHD. I don't want to sensationalize this—mice don't have ADHD—but they had problems with memory, impulsiveness and hyperactivity," he explained.

There have been studies in humans that correlate the amount of time pregnant women spend on a cellphone with their children's ADHD, Taylor added.

The findings cannot therefore be directly extrapolated to women, but they do indicate that cellphone exposure during pregnancy may have effects.

"But, these studies were largely dismissed because there are many other things that correlate with cellphone use," he said, "This study is the first one that shows that there is a cause-and effect-relationship," at least in rodents, he said.

However, while studies involving animals can be useful, experts note that they frequently fail to produce similar results in humans.

The findings cannot therefore be directly extrapolated to women, but they do indicate that cellphone exposure during pregnancy may have effects, Taylor said. "We need to start thinking about how much is safe in humans and limit that exposure," he said.

"I think we need to be careful about radio-frequency exposures in pregnant women," he said. "The radiation may have consequences for the developing brain."

The report was published in the March 15 issue of *Scientific Reports*.

During 19 days of pregnancy, Taylor's team exposed mice to radiation from a turned on—but muted and silenced—cellphone placed above the cage.

In another group, mice were kept under the same conditions but with a deactivated phone.

The researcher measured electrical activity in the brains of adult mice that were exposed to radiation as fetuses. In addition, they conducted psychological and behavioral tests.

They found the mice exposed to radiation tended to be more hyperactive and had increased anxiety and reduced memory.

The explanation for this finding isn't clear, Taylor said. It might be due to heating of the developing brain cells or electrical changes in these cells, he theorized.

Taylor noted that you don't have to be talking on the cell phone to be exposed to radio-frequency radiation: "There is always radiation transmitted as long as the cellphone is on," he said.

Speaking for the cellphone industry, John Walls, a spokesman for the CTIA–The Wireless Association, said that "the peer-reviewed scientific evidence has overwhelmingly indicated that wireless devices, within the limits established by the FCC [Federal Communications Commission], do not pose a public health risk or cause any adverse health effects."

Findings Remain in Preliminary Stages

However, some doctors believe that more study might be warranted. Dr. Francene Gallousis, a perinatologist at Northern Westchester Hospital in Mt. Kisco, N.Y., said that "I think there is something to all this, but I don't know exactly what it is or how concerned we should be right now."

"It can't be ignored—it needs to be looked into," she added.

Gallousis did suggest that to be safe, women should limit their exposure to cellphone radiation. She advised them to try to limit the time talking on the cellphone and to not leave it on if it doesn't have to be.

Dr. Nagy Elsayyad, an assistant professor in the department of radiation oncology at the University of Miami Sylvester Comprehensive Cancer Center, has looked at cellphone radiation and the risk for cancer. He also believes that it's still too early to tell if the effects seen in mice translate to humans.

"These finding are interesting, but very preliminary," he said. "This is hypothesis-generating research, so it's too early to jump to any conclusions, but it's worth putting research money into."

4

Call Me on My Mobile Phone ... Or Better Not? INTERPHONE Results

Rodolfo Saracci and Jonathan Samet

Rodolfo Saracci is the director of research in epidemiology at the National Council in Pisa, Italy. He also serves as adjunct professor of epidemiology at the University of Aarhus in Denmark, and is a consultant for the International Agency for Research on Cancer in Lyon, France. Jonathan Samet is a pulmonary physician and epidemiologist and currently the chair for the Department of Preventative Medicine and the Keck School of Medicine at the University of Southern California (USC), as well as director of the USC Institute for Global Health. He was appointed to the National Cancer Advisory Board in 2011 and has received the Surgeon General's Medallion in 1990 and 2006.

As the number of cell phone subscribers climbs to over four and a half billion, research on the possible adverse health effects caused by the electromagnetic radiation emitted by the device has become the focus of several large epidemiological studies. The International Agency for Research on Cancer (IARC) conducted the case-control study INTERPHONE to examine the brain cancer levels among mobile phone users, which resulted in important but incomplete results. As cell phone use was not widely prevalent until five to ten years before the cancer cases followed in the study were diagnosed (between 2000 and 2004), INTER-PHONE is hindered by its relatively short observation period. Uneven participation rates also likely caused result-skewing biases, and therefore the study is inconclusive. Until there are studies that go beyond the reach of the original INTERPHONE research, the risks of cell phone use will remain unknown.

Mobile phone (cell phone) use is increasing extraordinarily rapidly worldwide. There are now 4.6 billion mobile phone subscribers worldwide.[1] In many low- and middle-income countries use of cell phones has made communications possible in vast areas lacking cable connections. Increasingly, in high-income countries, cell phones have replaced 'land lines' for personal telecommunications. Users of mobile phones are exposed to electromagnetic radiation, which has long been hypothesized to have adverse health effects, including increased risk of cancer.[2,3] Research on biological mechanisms of cellular and tissue injury by electromagnetic radiation has been inconclusive, and consequently epidemiological studies have been the principal source of evidence on potential health risks of mobile phone use. Brain tumours have been of particular concern because the electromagnetic radiation generated by mobile phones passes through the brain when the phones are used without a hands-free device. To date, findings of diverse studies on mobile phone use and brain tumour risk have been reported with mixed findings, but with no clear indication of increased risk for cancer.[4,5] To provide needed evidence on the potential risk of brain cancer associated with mobile phone use, the International Agency for Research on Cancer (IARC) initiated a multi-centre case-control study, the INTERPHONE study, in 1998–99.

A much awaited report from this large international study on mobile phone use and brain tumours is published in this issue of the IJE.[6] A number of previous papers cited in the article reported only partial findings from components of the multicentre study, heightening expectations on what the full data set would eventually show. The component studies were relatively underpowered, but they exhibited a rather consistent and baffling reduced risk among cell phone users. We now have the complete results and the researchers' interpretation of them. The INTERPHONE investigators conclude that 'There were suggestions of an increased risk of glioma, and much less of meningioma, at the highest exposure levels, for ipsilateral exposures and, for glioma, for tumours in the temporal lobe. However, biases and errors limit the strength of the conclusion we can draw from these analyses and prevent a causal interpretation'.[7] This statement, as with a similar one ('. . .these biases and errors prevent a causal interpretation of the results.') at the end of the Appendix 2 of the article[8] added during the editorial process of revision, is both elegant and oracular. Similar to any oracle it tolerates diametrically opposite readings. If more weight is given to the first sentence, a conclusion is reached in favour of an increased risk, albeit not definitively manifest yet, from intensive use of mobile phones. Giving more weight to the second sentence leads to the conclusion that there are enough sources of errors in the study to dismiss the apparent elevated risks as not real. With equal weight to the two sentences, any conclusion hangs in the balance.

INTERPHONE shares with all studies previously carried out on mobile phones and cancer the inherent limitation that it can investigate only a short period of observation since first exposure.

Is there any way out of this ambivalence? INTERPHONE is the largest study yet carried out and published on mobile phone use and cancer. It includes 2409 cases of meningioma, 2708 cases of glioma and two series of, respectively, 2662 and 2972 controls matched by age, sex and region of residence. With the coordination of IARC it has mobilized investigators in multiple centres within 13 countries '... to determine whether mobile phone use increases the risk of [brain] tumours and, specifically, whether radiofrequency energy emitted by mobile phones is tumorigenic'.[9]

Not surprisingly, we end by calling for more research.

Certainly this is the question that scientists, people and public health decision-makers have in mind, as they seek assurance that mobile phone use is safe and not a cause of brain tumours. As defined by Lowrance,[10] 'a thing is safe if its risks are judged to be acceptable'. This definition implies a need for quantification of risk, the role of epidemiological research and a judgement of its acceptability in individual and societal contexts. The risk of main interest is lifelong use, possibly beginning in childhood—a pattern of exposure that cannot yet be studied. The now testable scientific question and that addressed by the INTERPHONE study is whether mobile phones increase the risk of brain tumours within the first 10–15 years of use, a question much less liable to generate unwarranted expectations about the evidence that the INTERPHONE study could actually deliver. In high-income countries, mobile phone use began in the 1980s but was not widely prevalent until the mid-1990s. The cancer cases in the study were diagnosed between 2000 and 2004. As a consequence, <5% (110/2409) of the meningioma cases and <9% (252/2972) of the glioma cases occurred >10 years since start of mobile phone use. None of the today's established carcinogens, including tobacco, could have been firmly identified as increasing risk in the first 10 years or so since first exposure. Ionizing radiation is a recognized cause of brain tumours but except for rare instances the radiation induced cases occur on average after 10–20 years since the time of first exposure. INTERPHONE shares with all studies previously carried out on mobile phones and cancer the inherent limitation that it can investigate only a short period of observation since first exposure; the distribution of exposure is brief and truncated leaving limited incubation time for an exposure-related cancer to develop. Hence observing no increase in risk would be reassuring but only to a limited extent.

As a multi-centric study, INTERPHONE has, however, the potential advantage of incorporating simultaneous replication, if there is no methodological heterogeneity across the centres. Consistency of results among centres, a key element for drawing causal inferences, can be immediately examined, rather than awaiting the accumulation of results from successive and separate studies. Overall, a consistent inter-country pattern of replicated reduced risk for both meningioma and glioma is shown in Table 6 of Appendix 1 of the INTERPHONE article,[11] whereas Table 2 of the article shows an equally consistent pattern of reduced risks for different metrics of exposure (regular use vs never regular use, cumulative call time, cumulative number of calls) with only three odds ratios (ORs) out of 50 above 1. These results are also in line with the detailed findings already published in separate reports, involving nearly half of the cancer cases, from some of the participating countries. On the null hypothesis that there is no association between mobile phone use and brain cancer, ORs fluctuating randomly above and below 1 would be expected, whereas the observed patterns of reduced risks, on average of the order of 30%, would have a tiny probability of occurring just by chance. Having ruled out chance and the possibility of a protective effect—absent any supporting biological evidence—less plausible than the possibility of bias from a variety of sources, bias stands as the most likely explanation of the observed results. As already noted,[12] this interpretation carries the uncomfortable consequence that the interpretation of any result of the study becomes problematic, unless the sources of bias are identified and their consequences quantified.

The authors have carefully pursued bias as an explanation of their findings via several routes. Confronted with a participation rate appreciably lower among controls (average for centres: 53%) than among cases (averages of 78% for meningioma and 64% for glioma), they asked a sample of participants (cases in 9 centres, controls in 11 centres) who had refused the full interview to respond to a brief questionnaire. Among both cases and controls, non-participants reported a lower lifetime prevalence of mobile phone use than participants. Since the participation rate among controls was lower than among cases, this pattern of response to the request for participation introduces a lower frequency of regular phone users among controls than among cases. Extrapolating the findings from this sample to the whole study population, the researchers estimated[13,14] that this selective non-participation bias may have led to a reduction in the ORs for regular use of 5-15%, potentially accounting for most of the bias observed (Table 2 of the article[15]) for meningioma [21%, 95% confidence interval (CI) 9-32] and glioma (19%, 95% CI 6-30). A substantiated downward and generalized bias implies that any observed increase in risk would be underestimated, independent of statistical significance. If this bias extends to those with the highest exposure, then an increased risk has been observed in spite of this downward bias. In the top decile of cumulative call time, the most comprehensive metric of exposure, the observed and probably underestimated ORs are 1.15 for meningioma and 1.40 for glioma (Table 2 of the article[16]). People in the top decile used a mobile phone for a total of ≥1640 h, still not a very intensive use by today's pattern: spread over 10 years, the lower limit of this category is about half an hour per day. Sensitivity analyses (bottom part of Table 4 of Appendix 1 of the article[17]) show that the increased ORs are fairly consistent among countries. They appear further increased (Table 5: 1.45 for meningioma and 1.96 for glioma) when the participant reported using the phone on the same side of the tumour, yet the systematically higher ORs for ipsilateral vs controlateral use, even at low levels of exposure, points to reporting bias and casts doubt on this latter result.

A second approach to bias investigation and correction is presented in Appendix 2 of the INTERPHONE article.[18] To avoid the problem of a lower frequency of regular users among controls (arising from non-participation), ORs were calculated taking the lowest levels of regular use as the reference category rather than non-regular use. This approach has been often employed in occupational epidemiology when risk is compared between people at various level of exposure rather than between exposed and non-exposed subjects, the latter being regarded as an entirely different group. The table in Appendix 2 of the article[19] shows that the ORs for meningioma are only slightly changed (cf. Table 2 of the article[20]), whereas those for gliomas are now mostly close to (and above) 1; the OR for the top decile of cumulative call time has increased from 1.40 to 1.82. The direction of these corrections, the size of which may be questionable (as discussed in Appendix 2 of the article[21]) speaks again in favour of a contribution of non-participation bias to the observed low ORs. A further reason for the downward bias may, however, lie in a different direction, briefly mentioned in Appendix 2 of the article.[22] Low risks have been a recurrent feature not only of the INTERPHONE study, but also of other studies of mobile phones and brain tumours, including a nationwide cohort study[23] in which non-participation was not an issue. Major clinical manifestations of brain tumours may not be long lasting but lesser symptoms, including occasional seizures, may develop over several years before diagnosis, as indicated by findings of increased risk of brain tumours in people with a hospital discharge diagnosis of epilepsy =8 years earlier, the risk progressively increasing as the interval between epilepsy and tumour diagnosis becomes shorter.[24] In addition, a nationwide cohort study using the same database as the cohort brain cancer investigation[25] found reduced hospitalization rates among mobile phone users for a variety of central nervous system diagnoses (Alzheimer's disease, vascular dementia, other dementia, Parkinson's disease and epilepsy) for time periods up to 10 years after starting phone use. One explanation is that mobile phone users may be a healthy group showing a 'healthy user effect' but a more likely one is that people with prodromal manifestations of neurological disease make less use of mobile phones. Along with non-participation this selection bias may also contribute to the downward bias in the INTERPHONE study.

We commend the INTERPHONE investigators for a rigorously implemented protocol and the careful exploration of bias. INTERPHONE clearly demonstrates that epidemiological research has to give major emphasis to bias prevention and control. For the time being, INTERPHONE's findings, interpreted in the context of prior studies, tells us that the question as to whether mobile phone use increases risk for brain cancers remains open. Given the relatively short time of observation since first exposure and the acknowledged biases we simply do not know the answer to this question. Some may interpret the results differently and most who have been awaiting the results of the INTERPHONE study will be disappointed by its mixed findings. Those upholding a precautionary approach to the extent and manner of use of mobile phones may find some support in the elevated risks noted in subjects with the highest exposures.

Not surprisingly, we end by calling for more research, given the increasingly ubiquitous use of mobile phones, rising use by children and the indication from some studies, including the INTERPHONE study, that mobile phone use may increase risk for brain tumours. One possibility to minimize selection and information biases, proposed previously by Rothman,[26] would track cohorts of mobile phone users with exposures documented via company records and outcomes ascertained through record linkage with cancer registries. Large cohorts would be required to investigate adult brain cancers that have an incidence rate in the order of 10 per 100 000 person-years but the advantage is that once established a cohort can be repeatedly followed up in time, updating exposure measurements in cases and a random control sample. This type of investigation overcomes the problem of case-control studies conducted when not enough time has elapsed since first exposure to make possible the emergence of long latency adverse health effects. This approach was blocked in the USA through litigation.[27] Another possibility would be periodic replication of multi-centric case-control studies, comparable with the INTERPHONE study in design, although the potential for bias would likely remain.

Fortunately, high-quality cancer registries are in place in many countries around the world and descriptive patterns of brain tumour occurrence can be monitored through careful and ongoing analyses to detect changes suggestive of increased risk from mobile phone use.

The tired refrain 'more research is needed' fully applies in this instance: without more research the public's question about the acceptability of cancer risk from mobile phones will remain unanswered.

Notes

1. International Telecommunication Union. Measuring the Information Society. Geneva: International Telecommunication Union; 2010.
2. International Agency for Research on Cancer. Non-ionizing Radiation, Part 1: Static and Extremely Low-frequency (ELF) Electric and Magnetic Fields. IARC Monograph 80. Lyon: International Agency for Research on Cancer; 2002.
3. National Research Council. Possible Health Effects of Exposure to Residential Electric and Magnetic Fields. Washington, DC: National Academy Press; 1997.

4. Ahlbom A, Feychting M, Green A, Kheifets L, Savitz DA, Swerdlow AJ. Epidemiologic evidence on mobile phones and tumor risk: a review. Epidemiology 2009;20:639-52.

5. Khurana VG, Teo C, Kundi M, Hardell L, Carlberg M. Cell phones and brain tumors: a review including the long-term epidemiologic data. Surg Neurol 2009;72:205-14; discussion 14-15.

6. The INTERPHONE Study Group. Brain tumours risk in relation to mobile telephone use: results of the INTER-PHONE international case-control study. Int J Epidemiol 2010;39:
675-694.

7. Ibid.

8. Ibid.

9. Ibid.

10. Lowrance WW. Of Acceptable Risk: Science and the Determination of Safety. Los Altos, CA: William Kaufmann, Inc; 1976.

11. The INTERPHONE Study Group. Brain tumours risk in relation to mobile telephone use: results of the INTER-PHONE international case-control study. Int J Epidemiol 2010;39:675-694.

12. Saracci R, Pearce N. Commentary: observational studies may conceal a weakly elevated risk under the appearance of consistently reduced risks. Int J Epidemiol 2008;37:1313-15.

13. The INTERPHONE Study Group. Brain tumours risk in relation to mobile telephone use: results of the INTER-PHONE international case-control study. Int J Epidemiol 2010;39:675-694.

14. Vrijheid M, Richardson L, Armstrong BK, et al. Quantifying the impact of selection bias caused by nonparticipation in a case-control study of mobile phone use. Ann Epidemiol 2009;19:33-41.

15. The INTERPHONE Study Group. Brain tumours risk in relation to mobile telephone use: results of the INTER-PHONE international case-control study. Int J Epidemiol 2010;39:675-694.
16. Ibid.
17. Ibid.
18. Ibid.
19. Ibid.
20. Ibid.
21. Ibid.
22. Ibid.
23. Schüz J, Jacobsen R, Olsen JH, Boice JD Jr, McLaughlin JK, Johansen C. Cellular telephone use and cancer risk: update of a nationwide Danish cohort. J Natl Cancer Inst 2006;98:1707-13.
24. Schwartzbaum J, Jonsson F, Ahlbom A, et al. Prior hospitalization for epilepsy, diabetes, and stroke and subsequent glioma and meningioma risk. Cancer Epidemiol Biomarkers Prev 2005;14:643-50.
25. Schüz J, Waldemar G, Olsen JH, Johansen C. Risks of central nervous system diseases among mobile phone subscribers: a Danish retrospective cohort study. PloS ONE 2009;4:e4389.
26. Funch DP, Rothman KJ, Loughlin JE, Dreyer NA. Utility of telephone company records for epidemiologic studies of cellular telephones. Epidemiology 1996;7:299-302.
27. Parascandola M. Science and law. Cell phone lawsuits face a scientific test. Science 2001;294:1440-42.

5

Cell Phone Cancer Risks Remain Unclear Despite Research Efforts

Sharon Begley

Sharon Begley is senior health and science correspondent at Reuters news service. Previously she was the science editor for Newsweek *from 2009 to 2011 and a science columnist at the* Wall Street Journal *from 2002 to 2007. She coauthored the 2002 book* The Mind and the Brain *and is author of* Train Your Mind, Change Your Brain, *published in 2007.*

The research thus far conducted on the health effects of widespread cell phone use has resulted only in confusion and inconsistencies. Despite the INTERPHONE study being the largest and most heavily funded research of its kind, the study's results were inconclusive and incomplete. Fears of the potential effects of cell phone use originated from a 1997 Australian study that exposed mice to mobile phone level radiation for an hour each day and revealed a 240 percent increase in lymphoma. Subsequent studies looking to repeat those findings, however, have found no definitive link between cell phone use and cancer. While the science remains murky, cell phone subscriptions continue to rise with no sign of the public restricting its use due to the device's potential health effects.

To get a sense of the total, complete, and utter mess that is research on the health effects of cell phones, look no further than a study of whether the ubiquitous gadgets raise the risk of brain tumors. "Interphone," organized by the World Health Organization's International Agency for Research on Cancer, was the largest (10,751 subjects, ages 30 to 59, in 13 countries), longest (10 years), most expensive (as much as $30 million), and most labor-intensive (48 scientists) study of its kind. That boded well for producing credible conclusions. Instead, Interphone found that using a cell phone *decreased* the risk of glioma (primary brain cancer) by 19 percent. Even in people who had used cell phones for more than 10 years there was no increased risk of brain tumors, with the exception of those who said they had yakked away for more than 1,640 hours. And the 40 percent increased risk of glioma in this group came with a caveat that is emblematic of this field: this elevated risk, the scientists warned, may be an artifact of "biases and error," not real. Things got so acrimonious among Interphone scientists that they delayed announcing the results, finally released in May, for four years.

Flawed Experiments Spell Danger for Public

There are many, many ways to screw up experiments on the biological effects of cell-phone radiation, and in 20 years of studies scientists seem to have used every one. The result is a confused public and nearly incoherent government policies that careen back and forth like a drunk after last call. In April, Maine legislators voted against requiring warning labels on cell phones. In May, San Francisco mandated them. A bill to be introduced in Congress would require warning labels nationwide and create a research program—but the last time the government called for studies that would "finally" answer whether cell phones pose a risk of cancer was in 1999, and since then all that's been accomplished are studies on how to do the studies. Society has never been good at making decisions in the face of scientific uncertainty (what do we do about possibly carcinogenic pesticides? About climate change?), but with cell phones the situation is even worse: it may be impossible to get definitive answers in a reasonable time about whether the radio-frequency radiation the devices emit will kill any of the 4.6 billion people who now use them.

Scientists who believe cell phones are dangerous have been throwing out hypotheses to explain away the negative results.

Confusion from the Start

The first big uh-oh experiment, done in Australia and published in 1997, exposed mice to the radiation typical of cell phones (about 800 megahertz to more than 2 gigahertz; this study used 900 MHz) for one hour a day for 18 months. The mice got lymphoma at 2.4 times the rate that unexposed mice did. The alarming finding set off a stampede of research. Two studies in Texas, in 1998, exposed mice to 2,450-MHz radiation for 20 hours a day, every day, for 78 weeks, finding no extra breast cancers compared with mice that weren't zapped. A 2002 study in Germany, exposing mice to 900 MHz, found no increase in breast cancer. A 2002 Australian study—900 MHz, an hour a day, five days a week, for two years—looked for an increase in lymphomas: nothing. The biggest set of animal tests—called Perform-A, it took eight years, cost $10 million, was organized by the European Commission, and announced results in 2007—found no evidence that cell radiation induces or promotes cancer in exposed mice or rats.

Tests of whether the radiation kills, slows, or otherwise harms sperm are also enough to give you whiplash. In 2003: "no evidence suggesting an adverse effect of cell phone exposure on . . . testicular function or structure"; 2005: "no support to suggestions of adverse effect on spermatogenesis";

2005: "a significant genotoxic effect on . . . spermatozoa"; 2007: "significantly higher incidence of sperm cell death" suggesting "that carrying cell phones near reproductive organs could negatively affect male fertility"; 2009: "significantly reduced percentage of motile sperm."

Scientists who believe cell phones are dangerous have been throwing out hypotheses to explain away the negative results. Maybe something about the unexposed animals raised their rates of cancer or sperm problems, so by comparison the exposed animals didn't seem to be harmed. Maybe the studies should have used pulsed, on-off radiation rather than a continuous beam, the better to mimic the way we actually use mobile phones, suggests epidemiologist Devra Davis, whose book *Disconnect: The Truth About Cell Phone Radiation, What the Industry Has Done to Hide It, and How to Protect Your Family* will be published next month. Maybe it matters whether the lab animals are zapped while in a device like a Ferris wheel or while running around in cages. On the other hand, if these details do matter, maybe that in itself is significant. "One could say that if [cell phones' inducing cancer] is a robust effect, then it should show up regardless of the setup," says Louis Slesin, who as editor of *Microwave News* has been following this issue since 1981. "But since we don't know the mechanism [by which cell-phone radiation might cause cancer], it's possible that by changing something we've eliminated the effect."

Scientists who dismiss claims that cell-phone radiation is causing an epidemic of brain cancer argue that there isn't any mechanism. According to textbook biophysics, only radiation that has enough energy to ionize molecules—that is, knock off electrons—can trigger cancer. (X-rays are ionizing radiation, with some 15 million times the energy of cell phones.) Cell phones don't emit energy great enough to ionize molecules in living cells. Their radiation is "far below the cancer energy threshold," notes physicist Robert Park of the University of Maryland, who often battles junk science. But whenever he makes that point in his What's New e-newsletter, he gets flooded with angry responses insisting there are other ways low-energy radiation can do harm. "I don't like cell phones and I don't like writing about cell phones," says Park, "but the damned issue just won't go away."

Science on Both Sides Is Inconclusive

Studies of the effects of cell-phone radiation on cells growing in lab dishes are also all over the map. A 1997 experiment found that mast cells exposed to 835-MHz radiation proliferated in an unusual way, but another experiment that same year found no increase in cell proliferation under exposure to 837 MHz. A 2004 study found no evidence of DNA damage in rat brain cells when they were exposed to on-off cell-phone radiation, but a 2005 study found breaks in DNA strands in human and rat cells when they were exposed to 1,800 MHz. A 2008 study at the Medical University of Vienna found that cell-phone radiation caused numerous DNA-strand breaks. But a university investigation found that its data had been fabricated. "After literally hundreds of studies, there is nothing approaching a smoking gun," says Peter Sandman, a risk-communication expert in Princeton, N.J. "Most experts look at this pattern [of no effect or a weak effect] and conclude the risk is either small or nonexistent. If it were big it wouldn't keep disappearing and reappearing from one study to the next."

Even scientists who believe we are conducting a vast and dangerous experiment on our brains by using cell phones concede that the balance of evidence, from both in vitro [in an artificial environment] and in vivo [in a living organism] experiments, indicates that cell-phone radiation does not alter DNA or chromosomes in a way likely to initiate tumors. "There is no denying that the majority of published studies on radio frequency radiation and the brain do not show any impact," writes Devra Davis. "The preponderance of the evidence shows that cell phone radiation has little biological impact." She attributes this to the ways scientists can cook the books to avoid finding an effect.

The question as to whether mobile-phone use increases risk for brain cancers remains open. We simply do not know the answer.

Studying humans hasn't clarified things. The first big epidemiology study, in Denmark, used government cancer registries and company records of cell-phone charges. It found no increased rate of brain cancer, the scientists reported in 2001. But almost none of the subjects had used a cell for more than 10 years; 92 percent used one for less than five years. Since the latency period between exposure to a carcinogen and the appearance of brain cancer could well be 30 or 40 years, the negative finding isn't completely reassuring. Also, the scientists lumped together all cell users, which could hide an effect that appears only at high exposures, and included no children or teens, who might be especially vulnerable.

The Interphone study, which studied people with brain cancers diagnosed between 2000 and 2004, was supposed to do it right. But its finding that using a cell phone decreased the risk of glioma suggests the study was somehow flawed, because there is no plausible biological mechanism by which using a cell phone can be protective. The most likely glitch: something skewed the statistics in a way that reduced the calculated risk of using a cell phone by about 5 to 15 percent, according to Jonathan Samet of the University of Southern California, who analyzed the study for the *International Journal of Epidemiology*. If the same methodological flaws (which have to do with the control group, the Interphone scientists concede) occurred in the calculation of risk for the heaviest cell users, then their increased risk is both real and greater than reported. The top 10 percent of users—about half an hour a day for 10 years—would have an 82 percent higher risk of glioma. With about seven new cases per 100,000 people per year, that translates into increasing the annual risk from 0.007 percent to about 0.013 percent.

On the other hand—and when it comes to cell phones and cancer, there is always another hand—the study might exaggerate the true risk. If people with brain cancer unconsciously inflate their usage ("I have brain cancer: I must have used my cell hours and hours every week"), it would create a false positive, linking brain tumors to heavy cell use. Indeed, heavy users did overestimate, the Interphone scientists found, with some subjects saying they used their cell five and even 12 hours a day. With these methodological and statistical questions unresolved, says Samet, "the question as to whether mobile-phone use increases risk for brain cancers remains open. We simply do not know the answer."

For now, most users aren't letting the warnings [about cell phone use] dull their cellular infatuation.

It's not clear whether anyone has the stomach for another years-long study like Interphone to try to find the answer. To do it right would require documenting phone use precisely with company records, and cross-linking those data with cancer registries. Another obstacle is that brain cancer is rare. You'd need to study some 9.6 million people to pick up an elevated incidence of even 20 percent. As for animal tests, this month the National Toxicology Program (NTP), part of the National Institutes of Health, is finally beginning the ones the Food and Drug Administration requested a decade ago. The NTP expects to launch the main studies—exposing animals to radiation for two years—in 2011, and to report results in 2014.

Without Hard Evidence, the Status Quo Is Upheld

In the meantime, we will keep using our cell phones. It is striking how little the suspected danger resonates with users. Sure, some don corded headsets or use Bluetooth, which reduce radiation exposure (if you switch off the Bluetooth between calls). Some have given up talking in favor of texting, which by keeping the phone at a distance reduces radiation exposure. A few users even heed manufacturers' warnings (buried in the instructions) about how far to keep a phone from the body: an inch for the BlackBerry 8300, for instance, and five eighths of an inch for the iPhone. It will be interesting to see whether labeling affects consumer behavior. The relevant spec is SAR, or specific absorption rate, a measurement (in watts per kilogram) of how much radiation is absorbed by biological tissue; this is what San Francisco will require be posted at the point of sale. The legal maximum SAR in the United States is 1.6, but SARs vary widely, with the Motorola V195 at 1.6, but the Samsung Freeform at only 0.48.

For now, most users aren't letting the warnings dull their cellular infatuation. "People don't need to read up on the studies to get the accurate impression that the experts simply aren't sure," says Peter Sandman. "When people are inclined not to worry [because we love our cell phones] this uncertainty becomes a reason for calm: 'Even the experts don't know whether it's dangerous or not, so why sweat it!' We really, really don't want to learn that there are health reasons to restrict our use of this miraculous invention. Uncertainty gives us a reason to stay unconcerned." And since the scientific uncertainty may never go away, the vast experiment we are embarked on won't either.

6

Epidemiology Is an Unreliable Way to Show Cancer Risk from Cell Phones

Dariusz Leszczynski

Dariusz Leszczynski is a research professor at the Radiation and Nuclear Safety Authority in Finland. He is a contributor to The Washington Times *and the author of a science blog, "Between a Rock and a Hard Place," for Communities Digital News at* The Washington Times *that focuses on the health effects of cell phone radiation. http://communities.washingtontimes.com/ neighborhood/between-rock-and-hard-place.*

When researchers first began to tackle the question of whether cell phone radiation could result in brain tumors, epidemiological studies were given top priority. After two immensely costly, disappointing, and inconclusive studies, the question of the effectiveness of epidemiology must be raised. Epidemiology as a method is too vulnerable to uncontrollable factors, is too costly, and is too slow to be a reliable and useful research tool to determine cell phone cancer risk.

Epidemiological studies are given the most weight in evaluation of human health effects. Therefore, when researchers started their effort to find out whether cell phone radiation causes brain cancer, epidemiology was given the most of attention—and the most funding.

However, and please let me play "devils advocate", is the epidemiology overrated?

Will epidemiology ever give us reliable answers concerning cell phone radiation and brain cancer?

Two High-Profile Studies Flounder

In 2010 and in 2011, two of the largest epidemiological studies on brain cancer were published. It appears that the time and money were used generously, but the studies failed to provide reliable answers concerning cell phones radiation and brain cancer. Flaws in the design of both studies prevented delivering conclusive answers.

It was 1999 when the largest case-control epidemiological study, INTERPHONE, was planned. At that time, optimists hoped that by the end of this project in 2004 we would know whether cell phone radiation causes brain cancer.

After several delays, INTERPHONE published the results of the glioma brain cancer study in 2010.

The results were confusing, to say the least. Use of the cell phone for less than 10 years seemed to have a "protective" effect, whereas the use of the cell phone for more than 10 years showed a small increase in glioma occurrence.

Several problems with the design of INTERPHONE were debated. By design, the INTERPHONE study was unable to detect brain cancer induced by cell phone radiation because of its long (over 10 years) latency period.

By design, INTERPHONE compared reliable information concerning diagnosed cancers with entirely unreliable information about exposures.

At the time of execution of INTERPHONE (2000–2004), cell phones were in common use for only a few years. There would be not enough time for the development and diagnosis of brain cancer if it was caused by cell phone radiation.

However, there was an even more important design flaw. The information about the extent of exposures to cell phone radiation was based on individual recollection of the subjects in the study. The study subjects were asked about their history of using cell phone, including how long and how many phone calls they made in the past.

It is a very unreliable method. Who of us remembers how many and how long calls made a few days ago? The study subjects were asked to recall cell phone use up to ten years before the study.

Therefore, by design, INTERPHONE compared reliable information concerning diagnosed cancers with entirely unreliable information about exposures. Such kind of comparison can not produce reliable result, as was seen in the confusing results of the study published by INTERPHONE in 2010.

In 2011, the Danish Cohort published another large study, evaluated in this column in December 2011.

Similarly to INTERPHONE, the Danish Cohort compared reliable information on diagnosed brain cancers with the absolutely unreliable information about exposures based not on the use of cell phone but on the length of subscription with the network operator. The study also contaminated the control group with the cell phone users.

Epidemiology is very expensive and takes a very long time to get results. Any flaw in the study design sets us back by ten or more years.

Again, as with the INTERPHONE, the Danish Cohort made comparison of reliable data on cancer with the unreliable information about exposures [which] cannot produce [a] reliable final result.

Brain cancer is a rare disease, somewhat in the range of around 10 cases per 100,000 people. It means that in order to reliably detect the change, which seems to be less than 50%

according to flawed INTERPHONE, tens of thousands of the study subjects should be analyzed. This is very expensive but not necessarily productive.

As shown by the experiences with INTERPHONE and Danish Cohort, large amounts of money (tens of millions of Euros) and ample amounts of time (over 10 years) were used and no reliable answers received.

Volunteer Studies Provide Viable Alternatives

In the current situation, with the above presented experience, should the epidemiology be the first kind of studies to use our scarce research resources? Epidemiology is very expensive and takes a very long time to get results. Any flaw in the study design sets us back by ten or more years.

Would we be we better off using the available funding for the human studies examining acute effects of cell phone radiation on physiology? This would, of course, include studies of the known molecular events leading to initiation and development of cancer. We still do not know if cell phone radiation triggers any such events in living humans.

Performing physiological studies on volunteers will provide information whether any known carcinogenic events are triggered by cell phone radiation. Depending on the result, we could act immediately by imposing preventive measures based on scientific evidence.

To provide such information, epidemiology will still need tens of years before it is able to perform effective studies, assuming that studies will be designed without any major flaws. Volunteer studies examining physiology and pro-carcinogenetic events would provide information much faster.

In this time of scarce resources, we need to make choices how to obtain, most reliably and expeditiously, information about the possible effect of cell phone radiation on brain cancer.

Based on the experience of the last 10–15 years, epidemiology does not seem to be the method of choice.

7

Cell Phone Radiation Research Is Marred by Politics and Money

Rob Harrill

Rob Harrill is the engineering writer at the University of Washington's College of Engineering as well as journalism professor at Edmonds Community College in Lynwood, Washington.

While conducting a study on the effects of microwave radiation on the brain, Henry Lai was contacted by the National Institutes of Health after it reportedly received a complaint of Lai misusing grant funds. Lai connected the incident to an ongoing controversy surrounding the cell phone industry, which he claims is attempting to discredit his research. Lai, having reported that certain microwave radiation frequencies could cause DNA damage to the brain cells of rats, found himself at the center of a debate with companies like Motorola and Wireless Technology Research, who he felt would only fund his work if he presented results favorable to the corporations. Lai and his colleague N.P. Singh claim that industry-sponsored research and independent research are presenting conflicting data, and without government sponsorship, no clear results will surface until sufficient time can present overwhelming evidence, possibly coming too late for many.

Henry Lai has a vivid recollection of his introduction to the politics of big science. It was 1994, and he had just received a message from the National Institutes of Health, which was funding work he was doing on the effects of microwave radiation, similar to that emitted by cellular phones, on the brain. He and UW colleague Narendra "N.P." Singh had results indicating that the radiation could cause DNA damage in brain cells.

The news was apparently unwelcome in some quarters.

Someone had called the NIH to report that Lai was misusing his research funding by doing work not specified in the grant (the grant didn't mention DNA). And the agency wanted to know what was going on.

"It really scared the hell out of me," says Lai, a research professor in the UW's Department of Bioengineering who earned his Ph.D. from the UW in 1977. "I was awake all night, worrying about it, wondering what to do."

In the morning, he sent a fax to the agency, explaining how the research fell within the parameters of the grant. The NIH accepted his explanation and assured him that all was well. "They are usually fairly liberal in that regard," Lai says. "To do otherwise would stifle the scientific process."

The incident, he says, was only the beginning in a David-and-Goliath conflict pitting him—and other researchers—against an emerging technology that would rapidly become one of the most lucrative and powerful businesses on the planet: the cell phone industry.

To this day, the cell phone industry continues to dispute Lai and Singh's findings.

Researchers and Industry Butt Heads

The controversy goes back to a study by Lai and Singh published in a 1995 issue of *Bioelectromagnetics*. They found an increase in damaged DNA in the brain cells of rats after a single two-hour exposure to microwave radiation at levels considered "safe" by government standards.

The idea behind that study was relatively simple: expose rats to microwave radiation similar to that emitted by cell phones, then examine their brain cells to see if any DNA damage resulted. Such damage is worrisome because DNA carries the body's genetic code and breaks, if not repaired properly, could lead to mutations and even cancer.

It's all about science, politics and money, and not necessarily in that order.

When the study was first published, a spokesperson from the cell phone industry said it was "not very relevant because they didn't use the [same] cellular frequency or cellular power."

True, responds Lai. But effects at one frequency could also happen at another frequency, and the exposure level in the experiment was actually lower than one can get from a cell phone. What it indicated was potential problems with the type of radiation the devices emit.

To this day, the cell phone industry continues to dispute Lai and Singh's findings.

"I don't believe any of those studies have ever been replicated," says Joe Farren, director of public affairs for CTIA-The Wireless Association, a Washington, D.C.-based industry consortium that provides $1 million a year in funding for cell phone research. "We believe you should follow the science. The science to date shows there is not a health risk associated with the use of any wireless device."

Technically, Farren may be correct about Lai's study, but that's because no one has tried to replicate Lai and Singh's exact experiment. And a 1998 experiment that used common cell phone frequencies did find biological damage in some cases. More recently, a European research effort by 12 groups in seven countries also documented DNA damage from cell phone radiation.

While Lai is the first to say there are "no solid answers" to the controversy over cell phones and DNA damage, there is "cause for concern" and more work needs to be done. Instead, Lai says, he and his colleague have been the focus of a campaign to discredit their research. Consider:

- Internal documents from Motorola in the 1990s point to an organized plan to "war-game" Lai's work.

- When a scientist in California published results that seemed to support Lai's findings, he lost research funding and eventually left the field.

- At one point, the director of a group created to manage $25 million in industry-donated research money sent a memo to then-UW President Richard McCormick saying that Lai and Singh should be fired.

- Federal money for scientific investigation in the field has dried up, supplanted by funding from the industry—funding that Lai and others say can come with restrictions so oppressive they hamper scientific inquiry.

The stakes, both in terms of potential ramifications and profits, are high. According to consulting firm Deloitte & Touche, the global wireless market is expected to grow to two billion subscribers by the end of this year. An overall dollar figure for the industry would easily be in the hundreds of billions, according to Louis Slesin, who as editor of *Microwave News* has followed the ins and outs of research in the field of bioelectromagnetics for more than 20 years.

"It's all about science, politics and money, and not necessarily in that order," Slesin says. "Henry and N.P. had the courage to buck the system, and they have paid dearly for that."

In preparing this article, some industry officials didn't return phone calls asking about Lai's work and the controversy surrounding it. Others said they didn't have specific knowledge of the original study and the events it set into motion—it was more than 10 years ago—but they characterized such research as outside mainstream findings, which they say show that wireless technology is safe.

Still others maintain that possible hazards from recent studies could be discounted because those studies focus on older analog phones, which send out a steady wave of radiation. Newer digital phones operate at a lower intensity, sending out a pulsed stream.

A Swedish study published last fall [2004] that tracked 750 subjects who had used cell phones for at least 10 years made note of that difference, and included the following caveat:

"At the time the study was conducted, only analog mobile phones had been in use for more than 10 years and therefore we cannot determine if the results are confined to the use of analog phones or if the results would be similar after long-term use of digital phones."

But it would be a mistake to use that to support a stance that digital phones are proven safe, according to Slesin. The problem, he says, is that pulsed radiation is more likely than continuous wave radiation to have an effect on living things.

"There is a lot of work out there showing that digital signals are more biologically active," Slesin says. "At this point, no one knows whether the enhanced biological activity might compensate for the weaker signals."

Researchers Face Restrictions and Funding Cuts

Lai, a soft-spoken bespectacled man with an understated sense of humor—he once deadpanned to a national television reporter that the most difficult part of his research involved getting the rats to use tiny cell phones—still expresses surprise at being at the center of the ongoing, swirling debate.

"I'm just a simple scientist trying to do my research," he says. He sees the path that led to controversy as marked by chance and serendipity.

A Hong Kong native, Lai earned his bachelor's degree in physiology from McGill University in Montreal and came to the UW in 1972 to do graduate work. He earned his doctoral degree in psychology and did post-doc work in pharmacology with Akira Horita. His initial research involved the effects of alcohol on the brain. He also worked on a new compound to treat schizophrenia.

A shift came in 1979. Bill Guy, UW emeritus professor and a pioneer in the field of radio wave physics, offered Lai a chance to do research on microwaves through a grant from the Office of Naval Research.

Motorola started working behind the scenes to minimize any damage Lai's research might cause.

The pair first examined whether microwaves can affect drug interactions (they can), then if there appears to be an effect on learning (there does). Then, in the early '90s, Singh arrived in Seattle. He approached Lai about joining his lab. "He was an expert on DNA damage," Lai recalls. "I said, 'Well, why not?'"

Singh is one of the world's foremost experts on a DNA analysis called the "comet assay." The assay gets its name from the appearance of a damaged cell. First, the cell is set in a gel and "lysed" or punctured. Then an electric current is run across the cell. When strands of DNA break, the broken pieces are charged. The electric current causes those pieces to migrate through the gel. As a result, a damaged cell takes on the appearance of a comet, with the bits of damaged DNA forming the tail. The longer the tail, the more damage has resulted.

With Singh's expertise now at hand, Lai decided to look at how microwaves affect DNA. Lai and Singh compared rats exposed to a low dose of microwave radiation for two hours to a control group of rats that spent the same amount of time in the exposure device, but didn't receive any radiation. The exposed rats showed about a 30 percent increase in single-strand breaks in brain cell DNA compared to the control group.

As Lai and Singh sought funding to conduct follow-up studies, word of the research began to get out. According to internal documents that later came to light, Motorola started working behind the scenes to minimize any damage Lai's research might cause. In a memo and a draft position paper dated Dec. 13, 1994, officials talked about how they had "war-gamed the Lai-Singh issue" and were in the process of lining up experts who would be willing to point out weaknesses in Lai's study and reassure the public. This was before the study was published in 1995.

A couple of years later, Lai got money from Wireless Technology Research (WTR), a group organized by CTIA to administer $25 million in industry research funding, to do some follow-up studies. But the conditions that came with the funding were restrictive. So much so that Lai and Singh wrote an open letter to *Microwave News* recounting their experience. The letter, published in 1999, cited irregularities in processes and procedures that the two called "highly suspicious."

"In the 20 years or so that we have conducted experiments, for a variety of funding agencies, we have never encountered anything like this in the management of a scientific contract," the two wrote.

WTR leader George Carlo responded with a six-page letter to then-UW President Richard McCormick, complaining of the "libelous" letter to *Microwave News* and "a pattern of slanderous conduct by these men over the past several years." The letter closed with a threat of legal action and stated that Lai and Singh should be fired from the project. An answering letter from Vice Provost Steven Olswang stated that the University "encourages legitimate academic discourse" and would not intervene in the dispute.

While Lai and Singh were attempting to do their industry-funded follow-up study, the industry was looking for another opinion. Motorola approached Jerry Phillips, a researcher who worked in a lab at the Veteran's Administration Medical Center in Loma Linda, Calif. He was investigating electromagnetic fields and their biological effects. The lab had done work with Motorola before, and Phillips was interested. He made a proposal and was funded.

Recent findings from overseas, more than 10 years after Lai's work, seem to finally be providing support for a closer look at cell phone radiation.

He sent people to Seattle to learn how to do the comet assay. And he decided to expose the animals in his experiment to actual cell phone frequencies. What they found were increases in DNA damage at some levels of exposure and decreases at others.

"That's not unusual," Phillips says. "It happens with chemicals. One dose can do one thing, while a higher or lower dose does the opposite. In this case, if you produce a little bit of DNA damage, you are stimulating the repair mechanisms and you could actually see a net decrease because the repair will be done. However, if you overwhelm the repair mechanism, then you could see an increase."

"Based on the data, I told them that we need to start looking at repair mechanisms," Phillips recalls.

Motorola disagreed. Phillips says he was told the results were not ready for publication, was encouraged to do more work, and was offered additional money to continue the experiment.

"I said as much as I would like the money, this part of the study is done," he recalls. "I said it's time to move on." The study was published in Nov. 1998. Once the findings were released, Phillips' source of funding dried up.

Since then, another group, working out of Washington University in St. Louis with industry funding, has tried to replicate the experiment, but without success. According to Lai and Phillips, that group is doing the study differently, including using a different technique to gauge DNA damage.

"They haven't properly replicated the work that Henry did, or that I did," Phillips says.

Industry vs. Government Funding

In the meantime, recent findings from overseas, more than 10 years after Lai's work, seem to finally be providing support for a closer look at cell phone radiation.

Last fall, the journal *Epidemiology* published research results from a Swedish group that showed an increase in a rare type of non-cancerous brain tumor among cell phone users on the side of the head where the phone was most often held.

In December, a pan-European organization released results from an extensive four-year study carried out by 12 research groups in seven counties. Known as the REFLEX study, that research found significant increases in DNA damage in human and animal cells exposed to cell phone radiation in the laboratory. While not a cause for alarm, the results, which have yet to be published, underline the need for further study, scientists said.

A spokeswoman for the UK-based Mobile Operators Association called the results "preliminary," adding that, "It is not possible to draw conclusions from this preliminary data."

In 2000, Sir William Stewart, former chair of a British group that looked into the cell phone debate issued a report urging "a precautionary stance" while scientific data is gathered. This January he repeated that warning, adding that children should not use the devices for the time being.

Industry spokesman Farren says his organization sticks to its position. "Any official precautionary measures need to be based on the science," he says. "The majority of studies have shown there are no health effects."

It's a point well taken, Lai says. However, what the science seems to say depends on how you quantify it.

There is no longer funding available in the United States that isn't attached to the industry.

Lai says there have been about 200 studies on the biological effects of cell-phone-related radiation. If you put all the ones that say there is a biological effect on one side and those that say there is no effect on the other, you'd have two piles roughly equal in size. The research splits about 50-50.

"That, in and of itself, is alarming," Lai says. But it's not the whole story. If you divide up the same 200 studies by who sponsored the research, the numbers change.

"When you look at the non-industry sponsored research, it's about three to one—three out of every four papers shows an effect," Lai says. "Then, if you look at the industry-funded research, it's almost opposite—only one out of every four papers shows an effect."

The problem, he adds, is that there is no longer funding available in the United States that isn't attached to the industry. Lai, for one, refuses to take any more industry money.

"There are too many strings attached," he maintains. "Everyone uses the analogy of the tobacco industry and what happened there. It's like letting the fox watch the henhouse." While the FDA administers cell phone radiation studies, the money comes from the industry, he adds.

Microwave News Editor Slesin says he has pondered why government funding isn't available. His hypothesis is that it's a matter of attitude.

"There is a view out there among many scientists that this is just impossible—the radiation is too weak and there cannot be any effects," Slesin says. "We all know that ionizing radiation is bad. Ions are more reactive, there's no doubt it can lead to cancer, it's nasty stuff."

The people who work with ionizing radiation see EMF radiation—that from electromagnetic fields—as a 97-pound weakling, he continues. They believe it's not capable of doing anything.

"Yet, when you see effects like Henry reported, especially at the low power intensities, you have to ask what is going on to cause this?" he says. "As long as that attitude remains unchanged, you won't get more funding and you don't get anywhere."

As a result, many U.S. scientists have moved on, either focusing on other areas or leaving the research arena altogether, relying on the rest of the world to pick up the slack. In Lai's case, he is pursuing other research directions, where he can get funding. The most promising involves artemisinin, a derivative from the wormwood plant currently used to treat malaria. Lai's research shows it has promise as a powerful anti-cancer agent. Late last year, the UW licensed the technology to a Chinese pharmaceutical company that plans to take it to human trials and, if successful, to market.

I don't know if there's a problem, but I think we owe it to society to find out.

Time Will Tell

After what happened in Loma Linda, Phillips and his wife left research altogether. They now live in Colorado Springs, Colo., where he works for a company that develops science curricula.

"I do have a lot of regret for those lost opportunities," Phillips says. "We were really in a position to develop some good basic understandings of how radio frequency affects biological systems."

It's an issue that desperately needs to be explored, according to Slesin. Right now, a solid understanding doesn't exist. If anyone says they absolutely have the answer, he cautions, absolutely don't believe them. "We are swimming in uncertainty."

And the issue becomes increasingly relevant with each passing day.

"We are making some fundamental changes to the electromagnetic environment in which we live," Slesin continues. "Soon entire cities will be online so you can take your laptop anywhere and be on the Internet. What that means is we will all be exposed to electromagnetic radiation 24/7. I don't know if there's a problem, but I think we owe it to society to find out."

In the meantime, Lai prefers to err on the side of caution. He doesn't use a cell phone and requires that cell-savvy family members use headsets. He doesn't see the problem as intractable, just one that needs serious attention. We engineered the technology, he says, and he's confident that we can engineer our way out of any problems. But first, we need to take a close look at the data and admit that there may be a problem.

Either way, the answers will come, given time, Lai says. The question is will we get those answers in the way we want?

"We see effects, but we don't know what the consequences are," Lai says. "With so many people using cell phones, we will eventually know. The largest experiment in the history of the world is already under way. We will know, in about 10 or 15 years, maybe."

8

San Francisco's Mandatory Cell Phone Warnings Are Misleading

William Alsup

William Alsup is a judge in the US District Court for the Northern District of California. He was appointed in August 1999 by President Bill Clinton. Before serving as a federal judge, he clerked for Supreme Court Justice William O. Douglas. Alsup is a graduate of Harvard Law School.

The San Francisco cell phone warning ordinance—which mandates warnings on the risks of cell phone use with posters, fact-sheets, and stickers—moves beyond the responsibilities of the city to inform its citizens of a potential harm. The fact-sheet is misleading in its overall impression that cell phones are dangerous and are not under the control of government safety limits. The poster and sticker both also overstate and do not contextualize their listed warnings. The city has conceded that no evidence exists to tie cell phone use to elevated cancer levels, and therefore has no obligation to mandate warnings to the public. Editor's note: A federal appeals court blocked the ordinance in September 2012.

The ordinance at issue is an amended version of a prior ordinance passed in 2010. That ordinance had two basic requirements, both tied to "SAR values." SAR means Specific Absorption Rate, a measure of the amount of RF [radio fre-

William Alsup, "Order on Motion for Preliminary Injunction," *United States District Court for the Northern District of California*, October 27, 2011.

quency] energy absorbed by the body from cell phones. It required cell phone service providers selling through a retailer in San Francisco to provide those retailers with the SAR value for each cell phone. In turn, it also required retailers to post those SAR values.

The Litigation

In 2010, CTIA [Cellular Telephone Industry Association] commenced this action against the City and County of San Francisco, alleging the original ordinance was preempted by federal law and seeking declaratory and injunctive relief. Thereafter, pursuant to its rulemaking authority, the San Francisco Department of the Environment released drafts of the warning materials and requested public comment. According to San Francisco, the user tips included in the original display materials "were taken directly from the FCC's [Federal Communications Commission] website" where the word "radiation" was used numerous times.

Subsequent to CTIA's filing of its lawsuit, the FCC modified its wireless-device fact-sheet and omitted any suggestion to buy a phone with a lower SAR value, stating instead that SAR was not useful for comparing phones and would be potentially misleading if used for that purpose. The new FCC fact-sheet added the following: *"The FCC does not endorse the need for these practices,* but provides information on some simple steps that you can take to reduce your exposure to RF energy from cell phones".

Early this year, CTIA filed a first amended complaint alleging preemption and violation of the First Amendment. Pursuant to a stipulation, San Francisco agreed to stay enforcement of the original ordinance and regulations until June 15, 2011, in order "to make substantive revisions to the disclosures required by the Ordinance and the accompanying Regulations".

The Revised and Operative Ordinance

Amendments were made to the ordinance to meet issues raised in the litigation. The stated purpose of the amended ordinance—the ordinance now at issue—was to "improve and strengthen the disclosures required under the original Cell Phone Right-to-Know Ordinance to better achieve this public health purpose." Requirements to disclose SAR values were removed from the amended ordinance, as were references to "radiation." The findings section of the ordinance stated that until the FCC and the scientific community develop a

> metric for measuring the actual amount of radiofrequency energy an average user will absorb from each model of cell phone. [I]t is in the interest of the public health to require cell phone retailers to inform consumers about the potential health effects of cell phone use, and about measures they can take to reduce their exposure to radiofrequency energy from cell phones.

On July 26, 2011, the Board unanimously enacted the amended ordinance. It has three main requirements. *First*, it requires cell phone retailers to "display in a prominent location visible to the public, within the retail store, an informational poster developed by the Department of the Environment". *Second*, it requires cell phone retailers to provide "every customer that purchases a cell phone a free copy of an informational factsheet developed by the Department of the Environment. [T]his factsheet must also be provided to any customer who requests it, regardless of whether they purchase a cell phone or not". *Third*, it states that:

> if a cell phone retailer posts display materials in connection with sample phones or phones on display, the display materials must include ... three informational statements, whose contents, and size, and format as printed, shall be determined by the Department of the Environment: (1) A statement explaining that cell phones emit radiofrequency en-

ergy that is absorbed by the head and body; (2) A statement referencing measures to reduce exposure to radiofrequency energy from the use of a cell phone; and (3) A statement that the informational factsheet . . . is available from the cell phone retailer upon request.

Section 1104 mandates the Department of the Environment to develop an informational poster, fact-sheet, and statements to be included in the promotional materials, and to issue regulations specifying the contents, size, and format for the materials.

At issue, in short, are a poster, a fact-sheet, and a sticker.

Section 1105 requires the City Administrator to issue a "written warning" to any person in violation of the ordinance and permits imposition of administrative fines, if thirty days after issuance of the written warning, the City Administrator finds that the person who received the warning continues to violate the ordinance. An administrative fine of up to $100 may be issued for the first violation, up to $250 for the second violation within a twelve-month period, and up to $500 for the third and subsequent violations within a twelve-month period. Violation of the ordinance is not a crime; the ordinance will be enforced only through administrative fines.

The Mayor signed the ordinance into law on August 3, 2011. The ordinance took effect on September 6. The ordinance required that, within fifteen days of the effective date or as soon thereafter as practicable, the Department of the Environment adopt implementing regulations after giving public notice and holding a hearing. The Department released its draft regulations on September 16 and scheduled a public hearing for September 26. Four days after the public hearing, the Department issued final regulations specifying the poster, fact-sheet, and sticker for in-store displays. At the hearing, San Francisco agreed to postpone the compliance date pending decision on this motion.

At issue, in short, are a poster, a fact-sheet, and a sticker. The poster, which is eleven inches by seventeen inches, states at the top: "CELL PHONES EMIT RADIO-FREQUENCY ENERGY." Below that are human silhouettes, one with a cell phone near an ear and the other with a cell phone near a hip. The poster depicts red and yellow circles radiating from the phones into the bodies. The silhouettes take up half of the poster and are the main feature. Below the silhouettes, the poster states: "Studies continue to assess potential health effects of mobile phone use. If you wish to reduce your exposure, the City of San Francisco recommends that you:

- Keep distance between your phone and body,

- Use a headset, speakerphone, or text instead,

- Ask for a free factsheet with more tips. Below this message, there is a reference to websites for the San Francisco Department of the Environment, the FCC, and the World Health Organization. A tiny statement that reads: "This material was prepared solely by the City and County of San Francisco and must be provided to consumers under local law" is viewable at close range on the top and bottom of the poster. The municipal seal appears on the poster.

The fact-sheet, which is a little over eight by five inches, states: "YOU CAN LIMIT EXPOSURE TO RADIO-FREQUENCY (RF) ENERGY FROM YOUR CELL PHONE." The same radiated silhouettes as described above dominate the fact-sheet. The fact-sheet next states: "ALTHOUGH STUDIES CONTINUE TO ASSESS POTENTIAL HEALTH EFFECTS OF MOBILE PHONE USE, THE WORLD HEALTH ORGANIZATION HAS CLASSIFIED RF ENERGY AS A POSSIBLE CARCINOGEN." A tiny disclaimer that the material was prepared by San Francisco, as well as the municipal seal also appear on the fact-sheet. The back side of the fact-sheet states:

> If you are concerned about potential health effects from cell phone RF energy, the City of San Francisco recommends:
>
> - Limiting cell phone use by children,
>
> - Using a headset, speakerphone or text instcad,
>
> - Using belt clips and purses to keep distance between your phone and body,
>
> - Avoiding cell phones in areas with weak signals (elevators, on transit, etc.),
>
> - Reducing the number and length of calls.

Subtexts elaborate on each recommendation. The websites listed above are repeated.

The sticker, which is one by 2.5 inches, states: "Your head and body absorb RF Energy from cell phones. If you wish to reduce your exposure, ask for San Francisco's free factsheet." Stores must affix this to their display literature for cell phones and must supply their own paste.

San Francisco expressly based its rule on the absence of a definitive study ruling out any and all risk of harm, stating: "It is the policy of the City and County of San Francisco to adhere to the Precautionary Principle, which provides that the government should not wait for scientific proof of a health or safety risk before taking steps to inform the public of the potential for harm". . . .

This order . . . presumes that a government may impose, out of caution, at least some disclosure requirements based on nothing more than the possibility that an agent may (or may not) turn out to be harmful.

This order, therefore, proceeds on the presumption that San Francisco may require disclosure of accurate and uncontroversial facts as long as the disclosure requirements are reasonably related to its interest in alerting the public to a possible public health risk and to its interest in suggesting precautionary steps to mitigate the risk. Applying this standard, the ordinance is sustained in part and disapproved in part, as follows.

The Fact-Sheet

The reader will remember that the fact-sheet to be given to customers is a little over five by eight inches. Its largest headline states: "YOU CAN LIMIT EXPOSURE TO RADIO-FREQUENCY (RF) ENERGY FROM YOUR CELL PHONE." This is followed by two large dark silhouettes of the human body, side-by-side, like the kind used as targets at firing ranges. These silhouettes are the dominant feature on the entire page. One has a cell phone beaming bold red and yellow circles into the head. The other has a cell phone beaming bold red and yellow circles into the hip and groin regions. These silhouettes are followed by medium-size print stating: "ALTHOUGH STUDIES CONTINUE TO ASSESS POTENTIAL HEALTH EFFECTS OF MOBILE PHONE USE, THE WORLD HEALTH ORGANIZATION HAS CLASSIFIED RF ENERGY AS A POSSIBLE CARCINOGEN." A tiny footnote then states that the material is prepared solely by the City and County of San Francisco and must be provided to consumers under local law.

The overall impression left is that cell phones are dangerous and that they have somehow escaped the regulatory process.

The back side has a medium-sized font beginning, "IF YOU ARE CONCERNED ABOUT POTENTIAL HEALTH EFFECTS FROM CELL PHONE RF ENERGY, THE CITY OF SAN FRANCISCO RECOMMENDS:" This is followed by five ideas to reduce exposure. In smaller print, the back side lists three websites where the consumer can "learn more." Once again, a tiny footnote states that the material was prepared solely by the City and County of San Francisco. The municipal seal appears on both sides.

On the fact-sheet, San Francisco has edited the mandated disclosures down to a few statements—largely accurate as far as they go—such as, to repeat, cell phones radiate RF (true); cell phone users are subjected to RF energy (true); the closer the phone, the stronger the RF energy (true), and so on. Given that the factoids are accurate or at least have some anchor in the scientific literature, it is hard to see why, subject to the criticisms below, San Francisco cannot require their disclosure so long as there is a plausible public health threat and so long as it is clear to everyone that the warnings come from local government and not from the store. Even the FCC has implicitly recognized that excessive RF radiation is potentially dangerous. It did so when it "balanced" that risk against the need for a practical nationwide cell phone system. The FCC has never said that RF radiation poses no danger at all, only that RF radiation can be set at acceptable levels. Given this implicit recognition of a risk and given the "possible carcinogen" classification by the World Health Organization, it cannot be said that San Francisco has acted irrationally in finding a potential public health risk and in requiring disclosures to mitigate that potential risk.

The image conveys a message that is neither factual nor uncontroversial, for cell phones have not been proven dangerous. The silhouettes are too much opinion and too little fact.

Nonetheless, the fact-sheet is misleading and must be corrected. Although each factoid in isolation may have an anchor in some article somewhere, the overall message of the fact-sheet (and the poster, for that matter) is misleading by omission in two important ways. The overall impression left is that cell phones are dangerous and that they have somehow escaped the regulatory process. That impression is untrue and misleading, for all of the cell phones sold in the United States must comply with safety limits set by the FCC. In other words, the uninitiated will be left with the misleading impression that the phones on sale have never been vetted by the FCC (or any other agency)—which, of course, is untrue. This would be misleading enough. But, even worse, the poster and the fact-sheet cite to the FCC's own website as if, should it be consulted, the overall misimpression would be confirmed. Once consulted, however, the FCC's message is very much the opposite. This overall misleading impression, however, could be corrected by adding a statement to the effect, "All cell phones sold in the United States must comply with RF safety limits set by the FCC" or, if San Francisco would prefer, "Although all cell phones sold in the United States must comply with RF safety limits set by the FCC, no safety study has ever ruled out the possibility of human harm from RF exposure." If this corrective item is unacceptable to San Francisco, then the entire program will be enjoined and San Francisco should broadcast its message at its own expense rather than compelling retailers to disseminate misleading statements.

A second misleading omission is the failure to explain the limited significance of the WHO "possible carcinogen" classification. The uninitiated will tend to misunderstand this as more dangerous than it really is because they will go uninformed that RF energy falls short of the "carcinogenic to humans" category and even short of the "probably carcinogenic to humans" category. To cure this misimpression, the fact-sheet should state, "RF Energy has been classified by the World Health Organization as a possible carcinogen rather than as a known carcinogen or a probable carcinogen and studies continue to assess the potential health effects of cell phones." Both corrections should be made in a font equal in dignity to that used throughout the fact-sheet, namely at least equivalent to the medium-sized font.

As for the large silhouettes with RF beaming into the head and hips, they are not facts but images subject to interpretation. One plausible interpretation is that cell phones are dangerous. This is not the only possible meaning but since the public might easily understand it in this way, the image must be scrutinized in that light. So viewed, the image conveys a message that is neither factual nor uncontroversial, for cell phones have not been proven dangerous. The silhouettes are too much opinion and too little fact. This is not cured by the writing elsewhere on the page, even as to be corrected. The silhouettes must be deleted.

The Poster

For the same reasons, the poster is likewise deficient but, more fundamentally, given that the fact-sheet is approved (with the corrections), this order finds that the large wall poster is not reasonably necessary and would unduly intrude on the retailers' wall space. All consumers who actually purchase a cell phone will receive the handout. There is no reasonable cause for requiring retailers to convert their walls to billboards for the municipal message.

San Francisco concedes that there is no evidence of cancer caused by cell phones.

The Stickers

The "sticker" requirement is also unconstitutional. Under the ordinance, if cell phone retailers put up their own display materials in connection with sample phones on display, as of course they do and will, all display materials "must include" a statement that cell phones emit radiofrequency energy that is absorbed by the head and body; a statement referencing measures to reduce exposure to RF cell phone energy, and a statement that an informational fact-sheet is available upon request. . . .

The stickers will unduly intrude upon the retailers' *own* message. Under the regulations, the mandatory stickers need not even state that the sticker message is solely the view of local government. But even if that were added (thereby enlarging even more the footprint of the sticker), it would still be unconstitutional to force retailers to paste the stickers over their own promotional literature. This would unduly interfere with the retailers' own right to speak to customers. Under the First Amendment, the retailers can communicate their message and San Francisco, within reason, can force the retailers to communicate its message too, but San Francisco cannot paste its municipal message over the message of the retailers. . . .

THE REMAINING FACTORS

The FCC has been studying radio since 1934 and based its cell phone emission standards on the "best scientific evidence available" after exhaustively gathering inputs from other federal agencies also concerned with human health. The FCC set a conservative standard, one weighted heavily in favor of minimizing any public health hazard. San Francisco has long been bathed in RF radiation from the Sutro Tower transmitting facilities, from radar, from hand-held television remotes, from portable phones, from WiFi (vigorously promoted by San Francisco itself), from WiFi-equipped notebook computers, from cell towers, from satellites, not to mention EMF radiation from our AC power infrastructure dating back a hundred years or more. If this exposure has been so dangerous, one might ask reasonably why hasn't it manifested itself by now? If there is a link, it must be weak or slow-acting. San Francisco concedes that there is no evidence of cancer caused by cell phones. San Francisco relies instead on its "precautionary principle," on the WHO classification of RF as a "possible carcinogen," and the argument that it should not have to wait until deaths start to occur to regulate. This presupposes that deaths *will* occur. But the evidence of impending death is weak. In weighing the equities, this must be considered. Put differently, no substantial public interest will be harmed by the preliminary relief granted above and the balance of equities favors it.

9

The San Francisco Cell Phone Ordinance Is Legally Justified and Prudent

Environmental Health Trust and the California Brain Tumor Association

The Environmental Health Trust (EHT) is a group of health professionals and communities that seeks to educate and advocate about threats to public health. EHT aims to mitigate the risks of cell phone radiation by stimulating research and encouraging policy changes. The California Brain Tumor Association (CBTA) is a nonprofit advocacy group that works to reduce brain cancer through school programs, independently funded research, community support, and participation in the making and maintenance of public policy.

The San Francisco Cell Phone Warning Ordinance is justified by a scientific consensus on the need for more research. The Federal Communications Commission (FCC), while being responsible for establishing the standards of safety regarding cell phone use, is unequipped to effectively measure the risks. Both national and independent researchers have concerns over the lack of evidence proving cell phones to be safe. The US Food and Drug Administration (FDA) notes that the effects of long-term exposure to radiofrequency energy remain woefully unknown. Studies in the medical field have posed questions of the risks of cell phone radiation causing brain cancer, targeting the developing cells of

Environmental Health Trust and the California Brain Tumor Association, "Amicus Curae Brief," February 1, 2012.

children, and endangering male sexual health. Editor's note: A federal appeals court blocked the San Francisco ordinance in September 2012.

Cell phones pose a potential danger to personal and public health because they emit RF (radio frequency) Energy, which has been correlated with negative health effects including an increased incidence of brain tumors, tumors affecting the acoustic nerve, and damage to sperm. The RF Energy emitted by cell phones causes thermal and non-thermal effects, the difference being whether heat is the mechanism; the federal RF Interagency Work Group and the Environmental Protection Agency are both concerned over the non-thermal health effects of RF Energy while the FCC [Federal Communications Commission] admits to not knowing if they pose a danger. Distance plays a key role in RF Energy absorption from near-field sources like cell phones, which is why the Ordinance's required factsheet suggests that a user text instead of call and make use of belt clips and purses.

World Health Organization Categorizes Risk

The WHO [World Health Organization], through the IARC [International Agency for Research on Cancer], "has classified radiofrequency electromagnetic fields as possibly carcinogenic to humans based on an increased risk for glioma, a malignant type of brain cancer, associated with wireless phone use." The IARC Director, Christopher Wild, states that "[g]iven the potential consequences for public health of this classification and findings . . . it is important that additional research be conducted into the long-term, heavy use of mobile phones. Pending the availability of such information, it is important to take pragmatic measures to reduce exposure such as hands-free devices or texting."

The Ordinance is an example of a pragmatic measure that addresses the interest of reducing exposure.

Importantly, the IARC's review of the scientific evidence included the industry funded and supported INTERPHONE study. "There were suggestions of an increased risk of glioma at the highest exposure levels . . ." despite no finding of a causal relationship. This positive relationship between high exposure levels and increased risk of glioma constitutes an unrefuted correlation and poses a potential personal and public health risk, especially considering the ubiquitous use of cell phones today.

FCC Is Unequipped to Function as Safety Agency

The FCC is responsible for establishing safety standards for cell phones, but the FCC is not a health and safety agency; for this reason, the FCC relies on the FDA [Food and Drug Administration] and the EPA [Environmental Protection Agency]. The current safety standards were established in 1996, only minor modifications have been made since. . . .

The FCC recognizes its lack of knowledge. In August of 1999, the FCC's Office of Engineering and Technology (OET) published an update of its Bulletin 56, which explains RF Energy, different biological responses to exposure, and many scientific nuances.

Bulletin 56 defines RF Energy, "Radio waves and microwaves are forms of electromagnetic energy that are collectively described by the term 'radiofrequency' or 'RF.'" The connection between RF Energy and cell phones is made shortly thereafter, "[t]hese waves are generated by the movement of electrical charges such as in a conductive metal object or antenna. For example, the alternating movement of charge (i.e., the 'current') in an antenna used by a radio or television broadcast station or in a cellular base station antenna generates electromagnetic waves that radiate away from the 'transmit' antenna and are then intercepted by a 'receive' antenna such as a rooftop TV antenna, car radio antenna or an antenna integrated into a hand-held device such as a cellular telephone."

The FDA explicitly states its concern over the unaddressed long-term effects of RF exposure.

Next, Bulletin 56 defines thermal and non-thermal biological effects. The thermal effects of RF Energy exposure are the "[b]iological effects that result from heating of tissue by RF energy. . . . It has been known for many years that exposure to high levels of RF radiation can be harmful due to the ability of RF energy to heat biological tissue rapidly. This is the principle by which microwave ovens cook food. . . ." The non-thermal effects of RF Energy exposure occur "[a]t relatively low levels of exposure to RF radiation, i.e., field intensities lower than those that would produce significant and measurable heating. . . ."

Regarding the FCC's agreement on the need for more research and recognized lack of knowledge, "[i]n general, while the possibility of 'non-thermal' biological effects may exist, whether or not such effects might indicate a human health hazard is not presently known. Further research is needed to determine the generality of such effects and their possible relevance, if any, to human health." . . .

Criticism from EPA and FDA Mount

The EPA found the 1996 FCC safety standards inadequate in several ways. First, they ignore potential non-thermal effects of RF Energy exposure. Second, they ignore potential long-term effects of RF Energy exposure. Third, they ignore the difference in risk for different parts of the population. Fourth, they ignore the difference in RF Energy absorption by different parts of the body (especially the head). . . .

The Food and Drug Administration (FDA) also commented on the FCC's proposed standards in 1993. The FDA explicitly states its concern over the unaddressed long-term effects of RF exposure. . . .

The City reviewed many studies that made the correlation between cell phone use and increased incidence of brain cancer and tumors affecting the acoustic nerve.

The FCC's 1996 safety standards ignore the potential personal and public health risk posed by the long-term use of cell phones. For these reasons, this court should uphold the district court in determining that the City's factsheet serves the interest of "protecting public health and safety" and extend this finding to the poster, sticker, and images. . . .

Studies Correlate Cell Phones and Brain Cancer

The City reviewed many studies that made the correlation between cell phone use and increased incidence of brain cancer and tumors affecting the acoustic nerve. These studies are in the supplemental record and, pertinently, they routinely conclude "[i]ncreased risk . . . for both cellular and cordless phones, highest in the group with >10 years latency period." Another found that, "[i]n summary our review yielded a consistent pattern of an increased risk for acoustic neuroma and glioma after >10 year mobile phone latency." Interestingly, the side of the head a person favors while using a phone may be a factor, "[f]or digital cellular phones no significantly increased risk was found overall, but ipsilateral exposure [the side of the head that a person favors] increased the risk significantly."

Children More Vulnerable to RF Energy

Supporting the Ordinance's suggestion to limit cell phone use by children, the City reviewed studies analyzing if children are more susceptible to RF Energy than adults. The WHO's IARC relied on this scientific evidence when it classified RF Energy as a possible carcinogen.

One study, which exposed phantoms (test dummies for measuring RF Energy absorption by humans) of both adult and child sizes, represents the scientific basis for the City to advise its citizens to limit cell phone use by children. The study concluded that "SAR [RF Energy absorption] results around 60% higher than those simulated for the adults were observed for the children with fitted parameters, independent of antenna type or frequency."

Male Sexual Health at Risk

Supporting the Ordinance's general concern "about the potential health effects from cell phone RF Energy," the City reviewed scientific evidence that (1) proves that when a cell phone's RF Energy is directly applied to sperm it causes a negative effect on sperm motility and (2) correlates a negative effect when a human male uses a cell phone regularly.

First, in a study applying RF Energy directly to a sperm sample outside the body, ". . . exposure to EMR [RF] led to a significant decrease in sperm motility." The study concludes by stating that ". . . statistically significant changes in sperm motility . . . was caused by the EMR produced by the cellular phone."

Second, in a study reviewing males, their phone use, and sperm motility, the seven medical doctors reviewing the data concluded that cell phone use correlated with decreased sperm motility. Specifically, "[t]he duration of possession [of a cell phone] and the daily transmission time [of use] correlated negatively with the proportion of rapid progressive motile sperm . . . and positively with the proportion of slow progressive motile sperm."

10

The Laws of Physics Make Cancer from Cell Phones a Virtual Impossibility

Bernard Leikind

Bernard Leikind is an independent physicist living in San Diego, California. A former professor of physics at the University of Maryland, he has contributed articles to The Guardian *newspaper in London and was senior editor of* Skeptic Magazine. *He has also served as a consultant on the Committee for the Scientific Investigation of Claims of the Paranormal.*

Cell phones emit a wattage of electromagnetic radiation of one watt, most of which is dispersed into the air. The waves that do pass through the body interact with molecules within a time span of about one billionth of a second. During this time, molecules are interacting with thousands of neighboring particles, thereby instantly dispersing the energy. Researchers have not outright declared cell phones to be safe because they falsely believe that the lack of evidence tying the devices to cancer is caused by faulty or limited research. It is clear, however, that the only effect of cell phone radiation is a slight increase in temperature.

Microwave radiation from cell phones cannot cause cancer by any mechanism, known or unknown. . . .

A cell phone emits about 1 Watt of electromagnetic radiation. Most of that zooms away to find a cell phone tower. The tissues of the user will absorb a part of this radiation. These tissues include the caller's hand, ear, scalp, skull, and brain. The closer a tissue is to the cell phone's antenna, the more of the radiation the tissue absorbs. For some reason, however, none of those raising fears about cell phones causing cancer are concerned about skin cancers on palms, fingers, or ears.

The frequency of the typical cell phone radiation is about 2.5 GHz, two and a half billion flips back and forth per second. The radiation travels at the speed of light—186,000 miles per second—and dividing the one by the other and correcting for the units I used for the speed, shows that the wavelength of this radiation is about 10 centimeters or about 4 inches.

As the electric fields of the waves pass through the body's tissues, the fields grab and try to shake any molecules or parts of the molecules that they can. These fields like to grab and shake water molecules, and there are plenty available. The fields will grab whatever else they can, which may be all or of parts of many of the critical molecules of biochemistry, such as the DNA in genes, or enzymes, fuel molecules, waste molecules, structural molecules, and so on.

If the cell phone's less than 1 Watt causes cancers, then why doesn't my exercise session's more than 1000 Watts cause cancer?

All of these molecules exist within the cytoplasm, and they are in close touch with one another. The molecules are quivering, twisting, and shaking, rattling about and transferring energy between each other. During the time—less than one billionth of a second—that it would take the cell phone's radiation to shake a molecule or part of a molecule back and forth, that molecule will suffer a thousand or ten thousand collisions with its neighbors. Any energy that the one molecule might begin to gather from the electromagnetic field rapidly spreads throughout all of its neighbors.

Coursing nearby to these molecules is a capillary filled with blood plasma and blood cells. This blood is at body temperature. Any extra energy from any source that appears in cells close to the capillaries will transfer into the slightly cooler blood, warming it. The flowing blood will carry the energy throughout the body. The body temperature will increase imperceptibly, and the extra energy will eventually transfer from the skin into the environment.

Anyone who puts forward a potential mechanism by which this energy flow, less than 1 Watt, might cause any cancer should notice that he has thereby explained too much. One watt is much smaller than many other natural energy flows that no one suspects might cause cancer. In my *Skeptic* paper, I show that the average energy production in my body as I go about my life is about 100 Watts. I also show that while I jog on my local gym's treadmill for half an hour, I produce 1100 or 1200 Watts. This energy, produced in my leg muscles, travels throughout my body including my brain, and I sweat a lot. My body's temperature does not change much. No one believes that my frequent treadmill sessions cause cancer. If the cell phone's less than 1 Watt causes cancers, then why doesn't my exercise session's more than 1000 Watts cause cancer?

Lack of Evidence Is Itself an Answer

Within the past year the results from two major epidemiological studies appeared in the scientific literature and to great fanfare in the media. Plainly stated, these two different kinds of studies found no evidence to link cell phones and brain cancers. The researchers might have simply said, "We did these large, carefully designed studies, and cell phones have nothing to do with brain cancer."

In the major Danish study, the researchers collected data from the entire populations of Denmark, Sweden, Norway, and Finland. These sensible countries have long provided medical care for all of their fortunate residents. Therefore, the researchers had access to thorough records. Brain cancers are rare, so they must search through large populations to find sufficient cases to draw conclusions. The plan of this study was to compare trends in the incidence of brain cancers from the late 1980s into the mid 1990s when cell phone use was non-existent or rare with the incidence in the first decade of the 21st century when cell phone use was wide spread. They saw no effect. None. Zero. Nada.

Physicists have solved the problem of microwave radiation and absorption. We know exactly what happens to the radiation, and there is no fuzzy area about it that we do not understand.

These researchers believe that cell phones must cause brain cancer somehow to some degree. Therefore, they asserted that perhaps their study was not large enough, perhaps their study did not cover sufficient time, or perhaps the large sample population diluted the effect in susceptible subgroups. They grudgingly admitted that it was possible that their study showed no effect because cell phones do not cause cancer.

The other study, known as the Interphone study, is a case-control study. Searching the populations of 13 European nations the researchers found 6000 brain cancer patients. Next, the researchers sought out 6000 more people to form a matched control group. Then the epidemiologists searched their data to see if they could detect suggestions that cell phone use might increase the risk of brain cancer. "The results really don't allow us to conclude that there is any risk associated with mobile phone use, but . . . it is also premature to say that there is no risk associated with it," the IARC's [International Agency for Research on Cancer] director Christopher Wild told Reuters. Also:

Data from the IARC study showed that overall, mobile telephone users in fact had a lower risk of brain cancer than people who had never used one, but the 21 scientists ... said this finding suggested problems with the method, or inaccurate information from those who took part.

Other results showed high cumulative call time may slightly raise the risk, but again the finding was not reliable.

"We can't just conclude that there is no effect," said Elisabeth Cardis of the Centre for Research in Environmental Epidemiology in Barcelona, Spain, who led the study.

"There are indications of a possible increase. We're not sure that it is correct. It could be due to bias, but the indications are sufficiently strong ... to be concerned."

No Grey Area

Why aren't these researchers proclaiming the brilliant discovery that cell phones protect against brain cancer? Why do they believe that concern is justified? They are confident that there is no possible way for cell phones to reduce the risk of brain cancer, but they suspect that the physicists might be wrong that there is no mechanism.

Physicists have solved the problem of microwave radiation and absorption. We know exactly what happens to the radiation, and there is no fuzzy area about it that we do not understand. The epidemiologists hear instead that physicists do not know of a mechanism by which the radiation might cause cancer.

The epidemiologists explain away their great discovery that cell phones protect against cancer and suspect that they may cause brain cancer because they believe the first has no mechanism and the second may have an unknown one. I argue strongly that there is no possible mechanism, known or unknown, by which cell phone radiation might cause cancer. However, the epidemiologists are wrong that there is no way by which cell phones might reduce the risk of brain cancer.

Here is my proposal. When our brains absorb energy from cell phones, there is a small temperature increase. When our bodies wish to energize our defense systems and to discomfit the bad guys, the immune system raises the temperature. If the problem is local, the innate immune system produces inflammation. If the problem is general, the innate immune system produces fever. Evidently, a slight, but noticeable temperature increase is beneficial to us.

Organizations to Contact

The editors have compiled the following list of organizations concerned with the issues debated in this book. The descriptions are derived from materials provided by the organizations. All have publications or information available for interested readers. The list was compiled on the date of publication of the present volume; the information provided here may change. Be aware that many organizations take several weeks or longer to respond to inquiries, so allow as much time as possible.

American Cancer Society

250 Williams St. NW, Atlanta, GA   30303

(800) 227-2345

website: www.cancer.org

The American Cancer Society is a nationwide, community-based voluntary health organization dedicated to eliminating cancer as a major health problem. In addition to advocacy, prevention, and patient support, it funds research into the causes and cures of cancer. Its website has numerous items on cell phone radiation and cancer.

American Physical Society (APS)

One Physics Ellipse, College Park, MD   20740-3844

(301) 209-3200 • fax: (301) 209-0865

website: www.aps.org

The American Physical Society (APS) is a nonprofit membership organization of physicists established in 1899. It works to advance and diffuse the knowledge of physics through its research journals, scientific meetings, and education, outreach, advocacy, and international activities. Some of its prominent members consider claims of cell phone radiation hazards to be unsupported by scientific evidence.

Committee for Skeptical Inquiry (CSI)

PO Box 703, Amherst, NY   14226
(716) 636-1425
e-mail: info@centerforinquiry.net
website: www.csicop.org

The Committee for Skeptical Inquiry (CSI) has as its mission to promote scientific inquiry, critical investigation, and the use of reason in examining controversial and extraordinary claims. Its website contains several articles casting doubt on various claims about cell phone radiation hazards.

CTIA-The Wireless Association

1400 16th St. NW, Suite 600, Washington, DC   20036
(202) 736-3200 • fax: (202) 785-0721
e-mail: info@ctia.org
website: www.ctia.org

CTIA-The Wireless Association is an international nonprofit membership organization representing the wireless communications industry. Established in 1984, its members include wireless carriers and their suppliers, as well as providers and manufacturers of wireless products such as cell phones. The association's website includes information about and links to various research studies that support the view that there is no correlation between cancer and cell phone use.

Environmental Health Trust (EHT)

PO Box 58, Teton Village, WY   83025
(307) 699-1912
website: www.ehtrust.org

The Environmental Health Trust (EHT) is a nonprofit organization founded by Devra Davis, author of *Disconnect: The Truth About Cell Phone Radiation, What the Industry Has Done to Hide It, and How to Protect Your Family*. Currently, EHT focuses on raising awareness on what it regards as unsafe cell phone use and the associated health implications.

Federal Communications Commission (FCC)

445 12th St. SW, Washington, DC   20554
(888) 225-5322 • fax: (866) 418-0232
e-mail: fccinfo@fcc.gov
website: www.fcc.gov

The Federal Communications Commission (FCC) is an independent US government agency, established by the Communications Act of 1934, and is charged with regulating interstate and international communications by radio, television, wire, satellite, and cable. It regulates wireless telecommunications, including cell phones.

International Commission on Non-Ionizing Radiation Protection (ICNIRP)

ICNIRP c/o BfS, Ingolstaedter Landstr. 1
Oberschleissheim   85764
   Germany
+49 3018 333 2156 • fax: +49 3018 333 2155
e-mail: g.ziegelberger@icnirp.org
website: www.icnirp.de

The International Commission on Non-Ionizing Radiation Protection (ICNIRP) is a European body of independent scientific experts. It includes committees covering epidemiology, biology, dosimetry, and radiation in relation to low-wavelength electromagnetic energy of the type emitted by cell phones. ICNIRP's website includes a link to its frequently cited INTERPHONE study, study updates, and links to research related to the study.

National Cancer Institute (NCI)

6116 Executive Blvd., Suite 300, Bethesda, MD   20892-8322
(800) 422-6237
e-mail: cancer.gov/global/contact/email-us
website: www.cancer.gov

The National Cancer Institute (NCI), established under the National Cancer Institute Act of 1937, is the federal government's principal agency for cancer research and training. It conducts and supports research, training, health information dissemination, and other programs. Its website includes policy statements and analysis of claims about cell phone radiation.

World Health Organization (WHO)

Avenue Appia 20, Geneva 27   1211
    Switzerland
+41 22 791 21 11 • fax: +41 22 791 31 11
e-mail: info@who.int
website: www.who.int

The World Health Organization, most often referred to as WHO, is the authority for health matters within the United Nations system. It is responsible for providing leadership on global health, shaping the health research agenda, setting norms and standards, articulating evidence-based policy options, providing technical support to countries, and monitoring and assessing health trends. In 2011, WHO put cell phone radiation on a list of possible cancer agents. The organization's website includes factsheets on the issue of cell phone radiation, as well as links to the INTERPHONE study and related research.

Bibliography

Books

Case Adams

Electromagnetic Health: Making Sense of the Research and Practical Solutions for Electromagnetic Fields (EMF) and Radio Frequencies (RF). Wilmington, DE: Logical Books, 2010.

Alex Berezow and Hank Campbell

Science Left Behind: Feel-Good Fallacies and the Rise of the Anti-Scientific Left. New York: PublicAffairs, 2012.

Adam Burgess

Cellular Phones, Public Fears, and a Culture of Precaution. New York: Cambridge University Press, 2003.

George Louis Carlo and Martin Schram

Cell Phones: Invisible Hazards in the Wireless Age—An Insider's Alarming Discoveries About Cancer and Genetic Damage. New York: Basic Books, 2002.

Carleigh Cooper

Cell Phones and the Dark Deception. Grandville, MI: Premier Advantage Publishing, 2009.

Kerry Crofton

Wireless Radiation Rescue: How to Use Cell Phones More Safely and Other Safer-Tech Solutions. Minneapolis, MN: Global WellBeing Books, 2011.

Devra Davis — *Disconnect: The Truth About Cell Phone Radiation, What the Industry Has Done to Hide It, and How to Protect Your Family.* New York: Dutton, 2010.

Ann Louise Gittleman — *Zapped: Why Your Cell Phone Shouldn't Be Your Alarm Clock and 1,268 Ways to Outsmart the Hazards of Electronic Pollution.* New York: HarperOne, 2010.

James C. Lin, ed. — *Advances in Electromagnetic Fields in Living Systems, Volume 5: Health Effects of Cell Phone Radiation.* Seattle: Amazon Digital Services, 2009.

Robert L. Park — *Voodoo Science: The Road from Foolishness to Fraud.* New York: Oxford University Press, 2001.

Kedar N. Prasad — *Radiation Injury Prevention and Mitigation in Humans.* Boca Raton, FL: CRC, 2012.

Camilla Rees and Magda Havas — *Public Health SOS: The Shadow Side of the Wireless Revolution.* Seattle: CreateSpace, 2009.

Periodicals and Internet Sources

BBC News — "Mobile Radiation 'Boosts Cancer Cells,'" October 23, 2002. http://news.bbc.co.uk.

Jennifer Couzin-Frankel   "Do Cell Phones Cause Cancer? An Explosive 'Maybe,'" *ScienceInsider*, May 31, 2011. http://news.sciencemag .org.

Devra Davis   "Cell Phones and Brain Cancer: The Real Story," *Huffington Post*, May 22, 2010. www.huffingtonpost.com.

Danielle Dellorto   "WHO: Cell Phone Use Can Increase Possible Cancer Risk," CNN, May 31, 2011. www.cnn.com.

Brenda Goodman   "Study: No Link Between Cell Phone Use and Cancer," *WebMD Health News*, October 20, 2011.

Dave Johnson   "Cell Phone Radiation Not Harmful (Says CTIA)," *CBS News MoneyWatch*, July 26, 2010. www.cbsnews.com.

Christine Kearney   "Cell Phones Pose No Health Risks, New Study," *Medical News Today*, September 18, 2012. www.medical newstoday.com.

Dara Kerr   "Link Between Cell Phones and Cancer May Be Unjustified," *CNET News*, April 26, 2012. http://news.cnet .com.

Deborah Kotz and Carolyn Y. Johnson   "Cellphones Are Added to List of Potential Risks for Cancer," *The Boston Globe*, June 1, 2011. www.boston.com.

Timothy W. Martin and Katherine Hobson	"Cellphone Cancer Warning," *Wall Street Journal*, June 1, 2011. http://online.wsj.com.
Nancy McVicar	"Study Finds Link Between Cell Phone Use, Rare Type of Brain Tumor," *Kansas Northern Star*, October 14, 2004. http://northern star.info.
Siddhartha Mukherjee	"Do Cellphones Cause Brain Cancer?" *New York Times Magazine*, April 13, 2011. www.nytimes.com.
Christian Nordqvist	"Mobile Phone Cancer Link Looking Less and Less Likely," *Medical News Today*, July 3, 2011. www.medical newstoday.com.
Benjamin Radford	"Was Sheryl Crow's Brain Tumor Caused by Cell Phones?" *Discovery News*, September 30, 2012. http://news.discovery.com.
Eifion Rees	"Do Mobile Phones Really Cause Cancer?" *The Ecologist*, June 7, 2011. www.theecologist.org.
Ian Sample	"Mobile Phone Radiation Is a Possible Cancer Risk, Warns WHO," *The Guardian*, May 31, 2011. www.guardian.co.uk.
Todd Shields	"Mobile-Phone Radiation Safety to Be Reviewed by U.S. FCC," *Business Week*, June 15, 2012. www.business week.com.

Lorne Trottier   "Are Cell Phones a Possible Carcinogen?" *Science-Based Medicine*, April 2, 2012. www.sciencebased medicine.org.

Bryan Walsh   "Cell Phones and Cancer: A Study's Muddled Findings," *TIME*, May 17, 2010. www.time.com.

The Week   "The Cell Phone-Cancer Link: A myth?" October 24, 2011. http://theweek.com.

Andrew Weil   "Cell Phones and Cancer: How to Stay Safe," *Huffington Post*, October 9, 2009. www.huffingtonpost.com.

Index